019323

KT-520-680

F/C

Hollywood Voices

edited by
Andrew Sarris

WITHDRAWN FROM STOCK

CinemaTwo

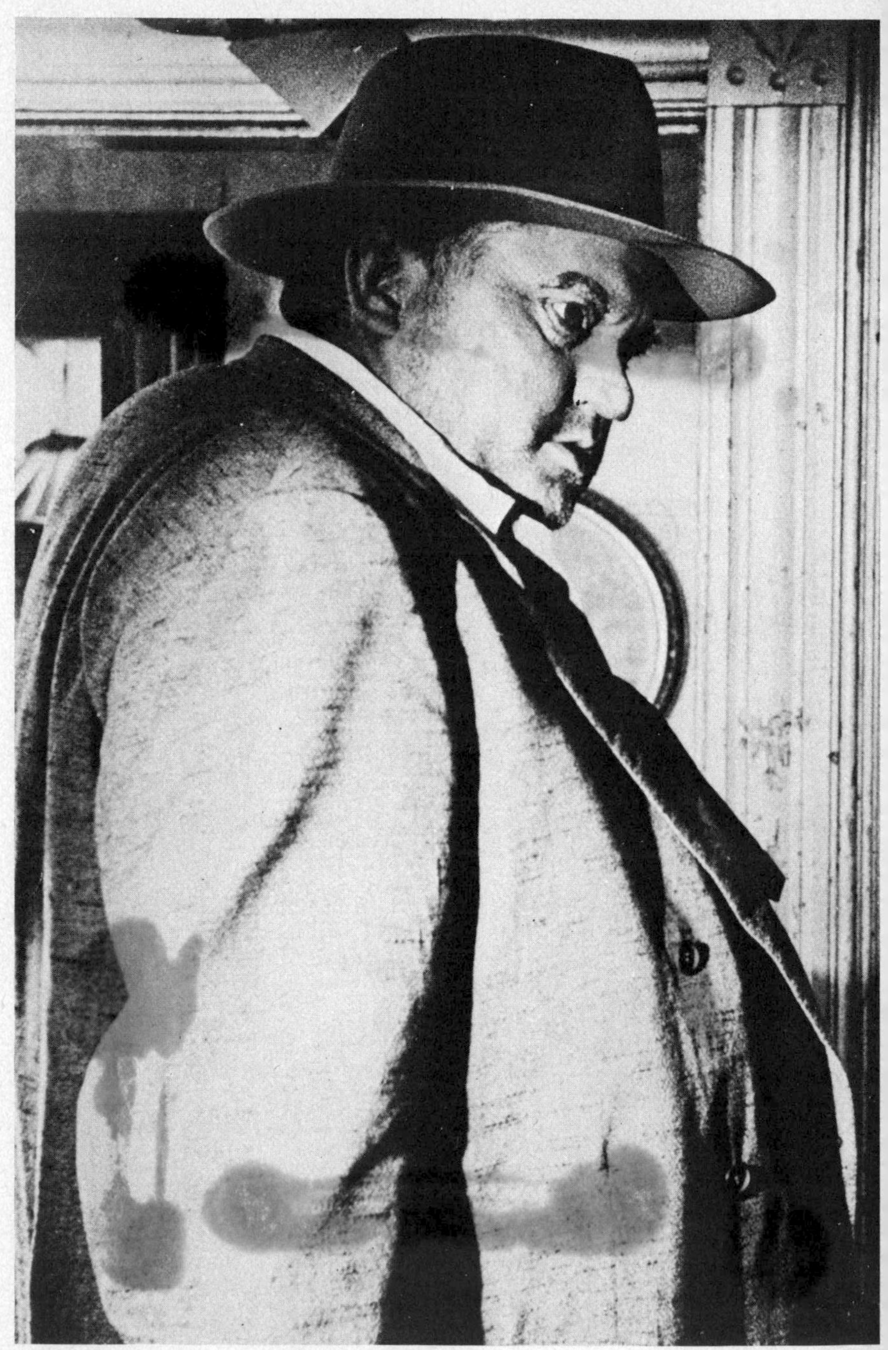

Orson Welles in *Touch of Evil*

HOLLYWOOD VOICES

Interviews with Film Directors
edited by Andrew Sarris

Secker & Warburg
London

THE LIBRARY
West Surrey College of Art and Design

This book is sold subject to the condition that it shall not, by way of trade or otherwise, be lent, re-sold, hired out, or otherwise circulated without the Publisher's prior consent, in any form of binding or cover other than that in which it is published and without a similar condition including this condition being imposed on a subsequent purchaser.

First published in Great Britain 1971 by
Martin Secker & Warburg Limited
14 Carlisle Street, Soho Square, London, W1V 6NN
Copyright © 1967 by Andrew Sarris

Adapted from *Interviews with Film Directors*
first published in the USA 1967 by
The Bobbs-Merrill Company Inc.

For this edition the checklists at the end of each section have been revised and a number of minor textual emendations made. The publishers are grateful to Miss Gillian Hartnoll of the British Film Institute for her help in this connection

All rights reserved. No part of this publication may be reproduced, stored in a retrieval system, or transmitted in any form or by any means, electronic, mechanical, photocopying, recording or otherwise, without the prior permission of the publishers

A Shadows Book
designed by Bentley/Farrell/Burnett

SBN 436 44151 9 (clothbound)
SBN 436 44152 7 (paperbound)

791.430973
SAR

19323

Printed in Great Britain by
Jarrold and Sons Limited, Norwich

Contents

Acknowledgements

For permission to reprint interviews with, and statements on and by the directors mentioned, the editor and publisher are grateful to the following:

Cahiers du Cinéma and *Cahiers du Cinéma in English*, © 1965 and 1966, for Welles.

Film Comment, © 1965, for Preminger.

Film Culture, © 1962 and 1964, for Sturges and Cukor.

Film Quarterly, © 1962 and 1965, for Polonsky and Huston.

Movie, © 1965, for Preminger.

Sight and Sound, © 1961, for Losey and Ray.

Stills by courtesy of: British Lion, Les Films du Carosse, Columbia, Gaumont-Distribution, Robert and Raymond Hakim, London Independent Producers, M-G-M, Paramount, Planet Film Distributors, Rank, Republic Pictures, RKO, Twentieth Century-Fox, United Artists, Universal-International, Warners.

The Rise and Fall of the Film Director

by Andrew Sarris

Greta Garbo's creakiest vehicle of the 30s was an opus entitled *Susan Lennox – Her Fall and Rise*. Film historians and archivists have repeatedly restored the classical cadence of 'Rise and Fall' to the title in defiance of the plot line and the aggressively American optimism it represents. Film directors are comparable to sudsy Susan Lennox in that their tarnished professional image has regained its gloss after a long period of neglect and downright disrepute. In fact, the renewed awareness of the film director as a conscious artist is one of the more interesting cultural phenomena of the past decade. This renewal can be described as a rise only in the most relative terms. The director has risen no more than the sun rises. As the latter is a figure of speech describing the diurnal rotation of the earth from the point of view of the fallible human eye, the pre-eminence of the director has been a matter of public and critical fancy.

Like the sun, the director has always been out there on the set, and his turn to be worshipped has come full circle from the earliest days of his solitary pre-eminence behind primitive tripod cameras pointed at a world still visually virginal. This intimation of lost innocence is invoked in Billy Wilder's *Sunset Boulevard* when Erich von Stroheim commands the newsreel cameras to turn on Gloria Swanson as she descends the staircase to utter madness. There is more than the numbing nostalgia for a burnt-out star in this sequence; there is also the evocation of an era when movie-making was more individual, less industrial. It is immaterial whether there ever was an era of directorial enlightenment. Many film historians have testified to the existence of a Golden Age in order to create a frame of reference. The gold may have turned to brass before 1925 or 1920 or 1915, but somewhere along the line, the legend persists, the film director lost all his freedom and integrity to some monstrous entity known as the motion picture industry – code name: Hollywood.

Confirmation of this legend of directorial decline and decadence has been provided by veteran Hollywood director George Stevens: 'When the movie industry was young, the film-maker was its core and the men who handled the business details his partner. . . . When [the director] finally looked around, he found his partner's name on the door. Thus the film-maker became the employee, and the man who had the time to attend to the business details became the head of the studio.'

Studio head Samuel Goldwyn put the matter somewhat more brutally when a reporter had the temerity to begin a sentence with the statement: 'When William Wyler made *Wuthering Heights*. . . .' The reporter never passed beyond the premise. '*I* made *Wuthering Heights*,' Goldwyn snapped. 'Wyler only directed it.'

'Only directed' is more precisely defined in the appendix of *The Film Till Now* by Paul Rotha and Richard Griffith: 'Director – (*a*) In feature films the Director is usually the technician who directs the shooting of the film, that is, he tells the players what to do and the cameraman what to shoot, and usually supervises the editing. Most feature films are directed from scripts written by the script department or by an independent script-writer. The editing is carried out by a department under a supervising editor working in consultation with the director and producer. Sometimes a director will write his own shooting-script and do his own editing; thus the film will tend much more to carry his individual mark.

'(*b*) In documentary films the Director usually writes his own script after first-hand investigation of the subject, although sometimes he may employ a dialogue writer. He not only directs the action of the film, but controls it through all stages of editing, music, dubbing, etc. War-time developments have tended to departmentalize documentary production as in story films.'

The most interesting aspect of this duplex definition, devised during the 40s, is its ingrained bias in favour of the documentary director.

Directors of 'feature' or 'story' films were presumably less artists than artisans not only because they were more closely supervised, but also because 'feature' films were considered more frivolous than documentary films. Thus, most movie directors were doubly denigrated in the scholarly texts of the period. On the one hand, most directors were charged with having too little control over their movies, and on the other, their movies were not considered worth doing in the first place.

Not that scholarly texts had any appreciable influence on the motion picture industry. Like so many other products of capitalism, movies were designed for immediate consumption and rapid expendability. Once a movie became 'old', it was returned to the vaults, never to be shown publicly again. Thus, even if there had been any interest in directional careers, the necessary research materials were not available. To make matters worse, film history was split in two by the advent of sound in the late 20s.

People who grew up in the 30s were completely unaware of the cinema of the 20s except for infrequent custard-pie two-reelers or an occasional revival of the foreign repertory – from *Caligari* to *Potemkin*. By about 1934, censorship had placed many movies of the early 30s out of bounds, a condition that existed until the 40s and 50s when television gold made it lucrative for studios to open their vaults. We are still a long way from the day when scholars can obtain the films they need from film libraries, but the proliferation of old films has had its effect on contemporary criticism. A greater awareness of the past, a sense of stylistic continuity in the works of individual directors, a cyclical pattern of period mannerisms – these are some of the dividends of the improved distribution of movies in the 60s. The most hardheaded businessman in the movie industry must now be at least marginally concerned with the burgeoning scholarship in the medium. By the same token, the most serious-minded scholar cannot avoid taking movies more seriously than heretofore, particularly when it is now possible to trace links between the Marx Brothers and Ionesco, between Buster Keaton and Samuel Beckett.

Unfortunately, most scholarly works on the cinema are still written from a predominantly sociological viewpoint, and most directors are still subordinated to both the studio and the star system that allegedly enslave them. Indeed most directors have always been considered less as creators than as decorators of other people's scenarios. That most directors do not write their own scripts is enough to discredit these directors in the eyes of the literary establishment. Such discredit is often unjustified even on literary grounds simply because many directors decline to take credit for collaboration on the writing of their films.

Furthermore, screenwriting involves more than mere dialogue and plot. The choice between a close-up and a long-shot, for example, may quite often transcend the plot. If the story of Little Red Riding Hood is told with the Wolf in close-up and Little Red Riding Hood in long-shot, the director is concerned primarily with the emotional problems of a wolf with a compulsion to eat little girls. If Little Red Riding Hood is in close-up and the Wolf in long-shot, the emphasis is shifted to the emotional problems of vestigial virginity in a wicked world. Thus, two different stories are being told with the same basic anecdotal material. What is at stake in the two versions of Little Red Riding Hood are two contrasting directorial attitudes towards life. One director identifies more with the Wolf – the male, the compulsive, the corrupted, even evil itself. The second director identifies with the little girl – the innocence, the illusion, thc ideal and hope of the race. Needless to say, few critics bother to make any distinction, proving perhaps that direction as creation is still only dimly understood.

As a consequence, contemporary film criticism has tended to diverge into two conflicting camps, the poor film director caught in the middle. First and foremost, we have the literary establishment, which relegates visual style to subordinate paragraphs in reviews. Then we have the visualists, who disdain plots and dialogues as literary impurities. Since most directors worthy of note work in the impure realm of the dramatic sound film, it is difficult to isolate their personal contributions to the cinema. The literary critics prefer to synopsize the plot, discuss the theme, if any, evaluate the performances, comment on the photography, editing, etc., and credit the director only for 'pacing', usually in the three speeds – fast, deliberate, and most often of all, too slow. Conversely, the visual critics concentrate on landscapes and abstractions as 'pure' cinema, and castigate dramatic scenes as 'talky', 'stagey', 'literary', etc. That is why the coming of sound was such a traumatic experience for serious film aestheticians of the late 20s and early 30s, and why much of what we call film history is actually the thinly disguised nostalgia of elderly film historians for the mute movies of their youth.

Through the haze of selective recollection, the silent film had apparently flown to an extraordinary elevation in the 20s only to crash through the sound barrier with a screech and a squeak. It became fashionable to mourn the tragedy of talkies until well into the 40s, and after to talk about the cinema in terms of artistic decline until well into the 50s.

The biographical pattern of almost every director went something like this: He started off very promisingly, but was soon corrupted by Hollywood (if he were foreign), or by big budgets (if he were American). His work became more and more 'commercial', less and less 'significant'. Because distribution was so erratic, it was always reasonably safe to say that yesterday's movies were superior to today's.

On the whole, however, directors were penalized more by critical indifference than by critical captiousness. Few people cared to read about directors; a volume of interviews of directors would have been inconceivable even as late as ten years ago. If the role of the director is now taken more seriously, it is because the cinema itself is taken more seriously. The director never really had any serious rival in the creative process. No one, least of all the serious scholar, was ever taken in by the pufferies of the producers. Selznick, Zanuck, Hughes, Goldwyn, and Thalberg did exercise great control over their productions, but few of their contributions were regarded as genuinely creative. Mostly, they maintained a certain level of technical quality in their productions, but production control without creative responsibility falls generally under the heading of interference.

The writer was even less serious a challenge to the director. Although the director was shackled to some extent by the studio system through the 30s and 40s, the writer was virtually deprived of his identity. As far as studios were concerned, there was never a question of too many scribes spoiling the script. Quite to the contrary, most producers believed strongly in the safety of numbers, and the multiple writing credits on the screen made it difficult for screenwriters to be taken seriously as screen authors.

By contrast, directors almost invariably received sole credit for their efforts, however craven and controlled these efforts may have been considered. In addition, the director's credit always appeared last on the screen – or almost always – one contractual exception being the aforementioned Samuel Goldwyn, a producer with a passion for having his name follow the director's. Nevertheless, the director's position, even in Hollywood, has always been strategically superior to the writer's. In the early 40s, the Screenwriter's Guild felt obliged to agitate for greater critical recognition, and the conflict became so exaggerated that, at one point, Stephen Longstreet attacked Vincente Minnelli for distracting audiences from dialogue with fancy camera angles in the 1945 Judy Garland-Robert Walker romance, *The Clock*. Needless to say, no screenwriter today would dare make a comparable objection.

Even today, however, the film director faces massive obstacles to critical recognition. Writers, actors, producers, and technicians challenge him at every turn. Also, the analogous and yet anomalous relationship with stage directors tends to confuse the issue. It is fashionable to say that the screen is a director's medium and the stage a writer's medium, but it is difficult to demonstrate that a Broadway-to-Hollywood-and-back director like Elia Kazan is any less in command in one medium than in another. To some extent, of course, the role of the director, stage or screen, depends on the person playing it. Many, if not most, film directors are little more than glorified stage managers charged with maintaining a schedule for the execution of the pre-ordained plans of the studio, the stars, the producer, the writer or writers, the technicians, the distributors, and even the vulgar public. At his least or his worst, the director is reduced to the level of a technician without the technician's pride in his craft. Such directors are like absolute despots compelled to act as constitutional monarchs, but lacking the style to conceal or circumvent their subservience.

At the other extreme, we have a new breed of film-makers who do not even call themselves 'directors'. These are the so-called independents, the 'poets', the perpetual *avant-garde* of the cinema. They scorn or pretend to scorn the elaborate technical and industrial processes of movie production for the sake of a more individualized creation. They are descended, if only atavistically, from the first film-makers, the curious cameramen who were playing with a new toy. Ironically, the *avant-garde* has generally resisted the stylistic and technological innovations initiated by so-called commercial movie-makers. Sound, colour, music, variable screens were all developed by the film industry while the *avant-garde* was publishing manifestos against them. The *avant-garde* has thus led the way not in form, but in content – anarchic, subversive, sacrilegious, scatological, and pornographic.

Through the years and decades, however, *avant-garde* attitudes in America have relied on the foreign 'art film' for intellectual authority. The Germans and the Russians were particularly fashionable in the 20s, before Hitler and Stalin stultified experimentation. Movies like *The Last Laugh* and *Variety* dramatized the expressive potentialities of the moving camera along with downbeat subjects considered too grim for Hollywood, but it was Sergei Eisenstein's *Potemkin* that galvanized a whole generation of intellectuals and aesthetes into wild enthusiasm over the creative possibilities of montage, a term that reverberated through the 20s and 30s the way *mise en scène* has reverberated through the 50s and 60s. Normally, montage is merely a fancy word for editing or cutting, but Eisenstein gave montage a mystique by linking it to the philosophical processes of dialectical materialism. As Eisenstein conceived of film-making, images equalled ideas, and the collision of two dynamically opposed images created a new idea. Eisenstein's montage theory was ideal for describing the collisions of the Russian Revolution, but there did not seem to be many other plots for which incessant montage was appropriate. The great majority of movies developed a dramatic style of expression to enhance audience identification with star personalities. Since in the world cinema the mystique of montage was thereafter honoured more in the breach than in the observance, film histories turned sour with acid critiques or alleged betrayals of the medium. As the gap widened between what was popular and what was intellectually fashionable, Eisensteinian aesthetics were supplemented by Marxist politics. Movies were not merely vulgar; they were instruments of capitalism in the never-ending class struggle. Film directors were thus presented with two choices: fight the establishment, or 'sell out'.

It remained for the illustrious French film critic André Bazin to eliminate much of the confusion arising from Eisenstein's half-digested montage theories. Bazin pinpointed psychological and physical situations in which montage disrupted the unity of man with his environment. Indeed it was French criticism in the late 40s and early 50s that introduced the mystique of *mise en scène* to counter-balance that on montage. The more extreme of Eisenstein's disciples had reached a stage of absurdity in which what was actually on the screen was secondary to the 'rhythm' of the film. The montage maniacs had thus enthroned punctuation at the expense of language. At times, it seemed that the camera was merely an excuse to get into the cutting room.

Ironically, the producers shared the highbrow enthusiasm over montage. 'We'll save it in the cutting room' became one of the hackneyed slogans of bad producers. *Mise en scène*, with its connotation of design and decor, reintroduced pictorial values to a medium that had become obsessed with the musical rhythms of images flashing by to be slashed on the moviola.

Because French critics were less awed by montage, they tended to be more appreciative of Hollywood than their cultivated counterparts in America and England. Most Hollywood directors of the 30s were disqualified serious consideration because they did not supervise the final editing (montage) of their films, for editing was then considered, by the aestheticians, the supreme function of cinematic creation. With the collapse of the montage mystique, however, many directors of the 30s have been rediscovered as undeniably personal artists. Not only do the best directors cut 'in the mind' rather than in the cutting room, but montage is only one aspect of a directorial personality.

Nonetheless, the Hollywood director is still taken less seriously than his foreign counterpart, and, in interviews, he generally regards himself with the same lack of seriousness. Part of his problem is the Hollywood ethos of the 'team'; part is the tendency of Hollywood movies to conceal the inner workings for the sake of popular illusionism. Audiences are not supposed to be conscious that a movie is directed; the movie just happens by some mysterious conjunction of the players with their plot. Quite often, Hollywood directors have laboured in obscurity to evolve an extraordinary economy of expression that escapes so-called highbrow critics in search of the obvious stylistic flourish. Consequently, there has been a tendency to overrate the European directors because of their relative articulateness about their artistic *Angst*, and now a reaction has set in against some of the disproportionate pomposity that has ensued. Some of the recent cults for Ingmar Bergman, Federico Fellini, and Michelangelo Antonioni create the impression that the cinema was born sometime between 1950 and 1960. Not that European directors are entirely to blame for occasionally appearing pretentious. They are merely playing the role that is expected of them, just as Hollywood directors are conditioned to pretend that they are all hardheaded businessmen. But here, too, the gap is narrowing as Hollywood directors venture to be more explicit about their artistic intentions and European directors dare to be more candid about commercial and professional problems.

As film scholarship becomes more sophisticated, the facile distinctions between so-called 'art' films and so-called 'commercial' films become less meaningful. Out of the sifting and winnowing emerges a new division of good 'art' and 'commercial' films on one side and bad 'art' and 'commercial' films on the other. Not only do art and commerce intersect; they are intertwined with the muddled processes of film-making. Even art films have to make money, and even commercial films have to make some statement. To put it another way, more and more critics are demanding that there should be more fun in art, and more art in fun. The post-Marxist pop and camp movements have perhaps overreacted to the socially conscious solemnity of the past, but the increasing scepticism about mere good intentions is a healthy sign of higher standards. Unfortunately, the pendulum has swung from the extreme of sobriety to the extreme of silliness. In the process, however, it has become possible to speak of Alfred Hitchcock and Michelangelo Antonioni in the same breath and with the same critical terminology. Suddenly every director is entitled to equal time on the international critical scene in which critics are compelled to abandon many of their cherished prejudices and snobberies. In a more open-minded atmosphere of critical recognition, it is only natural that film directors should abandon some of their defensive attitudes towards their roles. However, as instructive as the new frankness of film directors may be, interviews with directors cannot usurp the role of critical analysis.

André Bazin has summed up the situation admirably: 'There are, occasionally, good directors, like René Clement or Lattuada, who profess a precise aesthetic consciousness and accept a discussion on this level, but most of their colleagues react to aesthetic analysis with an attitude ranging from astonishment to irritation. Moreover, the astonishment is perfectly sincere and comprehensible. As for the irritation, this often springs from an instinctive resistance to the dismantling of a mechanism whose purpose is to create an illusion, and only mediocrities gain, in effect, from malfunctioning mechanisms. The director's irritation springs also from his resentment at being placed in a position that is foreign to him. Thus, I have seen a director as intelligent (and conscious) as Jean Grémillon play the village idiot and sabotage our discussion of *Lumière d'été* evidently because he did not agree with me. And how can I say he is wrong? Is not this impasse reminiscent of Paul Valéry leaving the lecture hall where Gustave Cohen has presented his famous commentary on *Cimetière Marin* with a word of ironic admiration for the professor's imagination? Must we conclude therefore that Paul Valéry is only an intuitive artist betrayed by a pedant's textual analysis and that *Cimetière Marin* is merely automatic writing?

'As a matter of fact,' Bazin declares, 'this apparent contradiction between the critic and the author should not trouble us. It is in the natural order of things, both subjectively and objectively. Subjectively, because artistic creation – even with the most intellectual temperaments – is essentially intuitive and practical: it is a matter of effects to attain and materials to conquer. Objectively, because a work of art escapes its creator and bypasses his conscious intentions, in direct proportion to its quality. The foundation of this objectivity also resides in the psychology of the creation to the inappreciable extent to which the artist does not really create but sets himself to crystallize, to order the sociological forces and the technical conditions into which he is thrust. This is particularly true of the American cinema in which you often find quasi-anonymous successes whose merit reflects, not on the director, but on the production system. But an objective

Jeanne Moreau in *Jules et Jim*

criticism, methodically ignoring 'intentions', is as applicable to the most personal work imaginable, like a poem or a painting, for example.

'This does not mean that knowing authors (*auteurs*) personally, or what they say about themselves and their work, may not clarify the critic's conception, and this is proven by taped interviews we have published in *Cahiers du Cinéma* through the 50s. These confidences, on the contrary, are infinitely precious, but they are not on the same plane as the criticism I am discussing or, if you will, they constitute a pre-critical, unrefined documentation and the critic still retains the liberty of interpretation.'

Bazin's actual acceptance of the director as author or '*auteur*' is typical of the French critical orientation towards the director as the sole creative artist of consequence in the cinema. Although the personal and poetic artistry of Ingmar Bergman and Federico Fellini in their films of the early 50s helped encourage a resurgence of serious interest in the cinema, it was not until the *nouvelle vague* emerged that the role of the director became fully romanticized for young people around the world. Bergman and Fellini were, after all, mature artists and remote figures to most of their admirers. Truffaut and Godard were young

Greta Garbo in *Queen Christina*

men in their twenties without practical experience. They were critics and enthusiasts, and they obviously loved movies with none of the dead chill of professionals. They also admired many of their predecessors, artists as disparate as Jean Renoir and Alfred Hitchcock. Above all, they had resurrected many directors from the limbo of low regard and had popularized the *politique des auteurs*, a mystique for reviewing directorial careers rather than individual films.

Overnight the director was king. Truffaut expressed the lyricism of being a director simply by freezing Jeanne Moreau on the screen, thus immortalizing her in a medium where montage implies mortality. Rouben Mamoulian did almost the same thing with Garbo in *Queen Christina* in 1933, but he could never go the whole way to freeze her, not because he didn't know how, but because the world of the 30s was not interested in how Mamoulian felt about Garbo. Mamoulian had been hired simply to present Garbo to her public. By contrast, Truffaut felt empowered to tell the whole world how he felt about Moreau. Jean-Luc Godard has been even more audacious in breaking every possible rule imposed upon a director by producers and aestheticians. If Godard has been abused for his impudence, Federico Fellini (*Otto e mezzo*), Richard Lester (*A Hard Day's Night*), and Tony Richardson (*Tom Jones*) have struck a post-*Breathless* bonanza by exploiting Godard's gimmicks to the hilt. The meaning of all the freezes, jump cuts, and zany camera speeds of the 60s is simply that directors have found the courage at long last to call attention to their techniques and personalities.

The interviews in this book do not in any sense constitute a definitive critical evaluation of the directors involved. The interviews are instead a kind of supplementation to the evidence on the screen. The film is still the thing, say what its director will, and it still takes more than giving a good interview to make a good film. The most articulate director in the world can also be the most inept film-maker, and, needless to say, the great master can be made to sound like a blithering idiot. In addition to the age-old barrier between the artist and the critic, there is the problem of a largely, though not entirely, visual art form being described in words, words, words. A somewhat frustrated film critic once observed that the only adequate critique of one film is another film. An extreme position, granted, but conversation under even the most ideal circumstances must remain secondary to creation. There will always be more (or less) on the screen than the most artful interview can express. More if the art is superior to its articulation, less if the articulation is revealed on the screen as mere rationalization. Perhaps Soren Kierkegaard anticipated the ultimate mystery of cinematic expression in *Either/Or*: 'I call these sketches Shadowgraphs,' he writes, 'partly by the designation to remind you at once that they derive from the darker side of life, partly because like other shadowgraphs they are not directly visible. When I take a shadowgraph in my hand, it makes no impression on me, and gives me no clear conception of it. Only when I hold it up opposite the wall, and now look not directly at it, but at that which appears on the wall, am I able to see it. So also with the picture which I wish to show here, an inward picture which does not become perceptible until I see it through the external. This external is perhaps quite unobtrusive, but not until I look through it do I discover that inner picture which I desire to show you, an inner picture too delicately drawn to be outwardly visible, woven as it is of the tenderest moods of the soul.'

Part One: Natives

Cukor, Garbo and Robert Taylor, during the shooting of *Camille*

George Cukor talking to Richard Overstreet, 1964

Even George Cukor's detractors concede his taste and style, but it has become fashionable to dismiss him as a woman's director because of his skill in directing actresses, a skill he shares with Griffith, Chaplin, Renoir, Ophuls, von Sternberg, Welles, Dreyer, Rossellini, Mizoguchi – ad infinitum, ad gloriam. *Another argument against Cukor is that he relies heavily on adaptations from the stage, that his cinema consequently lacks the purity of the Odessa Steps. This argument was refuted in principle by the late André Bazin. There is an honourable place in the cinema for both adaptations and the non-writer director, and Cukor, like Lubitsch, is one of the best examples of the non-writer author, a creature literary film critics seem unable to comprehend. The thematic consistency of Cukor's career has been achieved through a judicious mixture of selection and emphasis. The director's theme is imagination, with the focus on the imaginer rather than on the thing imagined. Cukor's cinema is a subjective cinema without an objective correlative. The usbands never appeared in* The Women, *and Edward never appears in* dward, My Son. *Most critics would argue that this merely proves ukor's slavish fidelity to his playwrights, but the fact remains that most ectors attempt to make plays more 'cinematic' by moving outdoors adding characters and extras. Not Cukor.* Bhowani Junction *and*

Heller in Pink Tights *demonstrate that Cukor is fully capable of exploiting exteriors when they serve his purposes. The opening Central Park sequence in* The Marrying Kind *is one of the most graceful exercises in open-air film-making in the history of the cinema, and the corresponding sequence in* It Should Happen to You *is not far behind. Yet, when characters have to thrash out their illusions and problems across the kitchen table, Cukor glides through his interiors without self-conscious reservations about what is 'cinematic' and what is not. It is no accident that many of Cukor's characters are thespians of one form or another. John Barrymore and Marie Dressler in* Dinner at Eight, *Ina Claire in* Royal Family of Broadway, *Katharine Hepburn and Cary Grant in* Sylvia Scarlett, *Judy Garland and James Mason in* A Star Is Born, *Jean Simmons in* The Actress, *Marilyn Monroe in* Let's Make Love, *and even Sophia Loren, De Sica's alleged earth mother, in* Heller in Pink Tights. *Even when Cukor's characters do not appear formally behind the footlights, they project an imaginative existence. W.C. Fields is pure ham in* David Copperfield, *and Katharine Hepburn is pure egoism in* The Philadelphia Story. *Cukor is equally sympathetic to the absurdities of both.* Les Girls *is Cukor's* Rashomon, *but where Kurosawa argues that all people are liars, Cukor suggests that all people tell the truth in their fashion. Even when imagination extends to transvestism in* Adam's Rib *and* Sylvia Scarlett, *Cukor retains an indulgent affection for the misguided brashness of Katharine Hepburn. The theme is consistent; the pattern is established. Cukor is committed to the dreamer, if not to the content of the dream. He is a genuine artist.* – A.S.

CUKOR: You know, there's nothing worse than making excuses. For example, saying when a picture hasn't gone well or when you've been badly reviewed that it was so-and-so's fault. What I do is just make a blanket statement: it was just an unfortunate thing and let's forget it. But since you're going into detail I will tell you about something. Curiously enough, some of the best scenes I've ever had anything to do with are in pictures that did not succeed. That is odd. But unless the story line carries the scenes the scenes really don't mean anything. I believe the story is frightfully important. Simple story telling. Without it you get a most beautiful production, most beautiful acting . . . but it's all ineffective because you don't arrest the attention of the audience.

OVERSTREET: *Do you feel that* The Chapman Report *was a success in this respect?*

I must tell you about that. It was the story of three women and their problems. With Jane Fonda the problem was frigidity . . . well, basic problem was that it was a rather lurid book and I believe the author, after a while, threw caution to the wind. So the whole ending is very hectic. But the book diverted me, nevertheless.

Did you read it before they asked you to do the picture?

I read it before . . . and I will say that I was influenced by one thing: I had an obligation to Fox. They were planning to sue me or some damn thing so I thought: let's just get this over with. But the story did interest me. It amused me greatly.

It must have . . . for, after all, it is a story about women.

Yes . . . about women. Sort of a cheapish story, really, but I thought it could be filmed without any vulgarity, you see. The book is full of it. . . .

The Jane Fonda episode was extremely interesting and much more complete than the others. You saw her run the gamut of experiences. You saw her try all these things: she goes into a motel with a man and draws back when he approaches her. And the Shelley Winters thing: she performed it well but she was rather vulgar. I was especially careful with the Claire Bloom part. There were moments when she had aspirations of some kind and you should have felt that she was a rather noble woman doing ignoble things.

Of the four actresses, were you most content with her performance?

Well, it was certainly the most complete. When the thing was all put together we took it up to San Francisco for a sneak preview and it went very well. It was quite interesting because the screening was in a theatre on Market Street and there was a rather nondescript crowd there. But I felt that the crowd was actually ahead of us. They had heard of the book. Thought it was very sexy. We could have gone even farther with the audience – not hedged at all with the touchy parts. I don't mean we should have been erotic, just more frank.

The preview was a very good one . . . but before I go on I should give you a little background. The picture was to be released by Warners but it was produced by Zanuck. Zanuck, however, was here in Europe shooting *The Longest Day*. He was a friend of mine, Zanuck. We got on very well together and his son was acting as producer. I was very nice to the son.

After the preview I made some minor suggestions about re-cutting, ıst re-working it a little. Then with these suggestions we shipped e print over to Zanuck. He then, as usual, cut the damned thing, mpletely re-cut it so that it no longer made any sense at all. He asculated it.

What are the major changes that he made?

He just cut everything every sort of mad way, that's all. When he brought it back to Warners it was absolutely incoherent. He did all this revising while he had *Longest Day* going. He was cutting the poor *Chapman Report* to bits and at the same time sending me ecstatic wires declaring how great it was. Then I learned that he was 'fixing it up'. At that point I refused to see the cut version. Warners were appalled at what he had done. Finally, I spoke to him, told him what I thought and he replied: 'Let's preview it just once my way to see how it goes.' I agreed – what else could I do? Warners restored certain things after Zanuck's re-working and while they were doing this I said to them: 'You know, if you cut out the high-minded parts of this thing the censors will jump down your throat because of the book's bad reputation. That is why we cast Claire Bloom. The part had to played on a high level.'

Zanuck said, 'I promise you on my word of honour . . . here's my son to bear me out . . . we'll preview it once with the re-cut version that I did, then we'll preview it your way.' That was that. There was to be no nonsense. The next thing I knew I was holding a wire in my hands: 'I find there is a clause in the contract. We don't have time for the previews. The picture must be released immediately so the last cut print will have to go out.' I wrote Zanuck a very indignant wire, then he sent me one back, very long and very nasty. He said that some ex-prizefighter friend of his had seen his version and thought it was great.

Then the censors jumped on our backs, made us cut the hell out of the picture . . .

Was Glynis Johns's part cut up by the censors – the erotic implications here being of a comic sort?

Her episode was completely different from the book – and surprisingly enough the only one which was very little hurt by the censors. So this pushed the whole thing out of proportion. Originally, she had a comic-minor role and coming out of the ordeal unscathed she was the only one who remained coherent . . . but much too important. The others were absolutely unbelievable, incoherent. At best, the film was not a masterpiece but in its original form it was amusing and slick and would have done well. But every quality it ever had was ripped out. It was ruined. Ruined.

Even though it was cut and desecrated your tasteful handling of the subject still came through.

Yes, it was in 'good taste'.

We had three . . . two very appetizing girls. Shelley Winters was, v

'laire Bloom in *The Chapman Report*

ll right. We decided that her hair was to be dark in the picture, then he gradually snuck this peroxide effect in. Before we knew it she had nade herself into a brassy blonde. It was too late to do anything about t . . . a stupid move. She did play some scenes with a great deal of eeling. . . .

The picture really was ruined. They said they made a lot of money. 'here would have been a lot of money in their pockets if they would ave left the picture as it was. As you know it was received with the reatest contempt in England. There is this man there by the name of 'revelyan who is the czar of what people see and what they don't see. Ie said it was vulgar . . . so that was the end of *The Chapman Report* in ngland. The whole thing was a complete disaster from beginning to nd.

With all these cutting problems – and they weren't the first such run-ins 'ou've had with producers – why didn't you produce sooner?

For many years I was under contract to Metro. There were hang-vers from old commitments which I had made and I just wasn't free. 1en when *My Fair Lady* came along I took that because I thought it was a great *coup*. I liked the idea of doing it even if I wasn't pro ducing. But now I definitely will produce on my own.

In the past there have been pictures marred by disagreements. Fo instance, there was *The Actress* with a scenario by Ruth Gordon base on her play *Years Ago*. The producer made some minor cuts and the had an *enormous* effect on the picture. Ruth was very pained by i because they changed the whole sense of the film. Jean Simmons playing Ruth as a girl, had the wilfulness, the slight ruthlessness of a actress. But in the cutting, slight as it was, her strength was mitigated her character was completely changed. Ruth was very pained by th slices and I agree with her.

The curious thing is when you're making a picture there's dam little help from others on the set. You've got this piece of paper i front of you . . . and the actors . . . and that's all. There's no one ther with the clever advice but when the thing's all over there are hundred of stooges all around telling you to cut this and that. Actually, the don't know a thing, those people, and I would hate any picture to hav to go through the emasculation that this poor *Chapman Report* wen through.

But The Chapman Report *wasn't as butchered as* A Star Is Born *was it?*

No . . . no. They just hacked into that one. Junked it completely Bits were cut and lost . . . very painful, indeed. Bosley Crowther wrot an article called 'A Star Is Shorn' . . . and it was, in fact! Things wer taken out and the negative corresponding to them were lost. complete disaster.

There were some terribly funny scenes that fell out. At the beginnin when Judy Garland and James Mason go out to the oil wells in a Lo Angeles suburb – she's still unknown then and he's the great star. It' night, they have a little conversation, he's in love with her, she's move . . . very moved by him, but the smell of the oil is just too much and sh gets sick; she's so humiliated.

The picture was, in fact, too long. But while I wasn't there the produced a big production number right in the middle – 'Born in Trunk'. It went on and on and in the context of the final cut versio was way too long. If they thought it was too long there were other way of shortening it besides chopping and hacking out vital bits. Had w been allowed, Moss Hart and I could have sweated out twenty minute which would have been imperceptible to the audience. That's some thing which I can't understand. Producers spend millions of dollars t do pictures and then suddenly, right out of the blue, they say: 'Le chop this out, then that. . . .' In what other business does this happen? I'm sure at Ford they don't make models of some car and then just throw them out.

It's very painful, all this. Fanny Brice, who was a wonderful woman and a great friend of mine, once said, 'The older we get, kid, the less you can brush off them knocks.' And she was right. The older you get the less you can. But there are some things I won't stand for, old or not. For example, when you're filming and there comes a moment of indecision – the people around you say: 'O.K., let's do it both ways . . . do the scene both ways and you can't go wrong.' I refuse point-blank and say that there is only one way to do it: let's decide what is the correct way and after there will be no alternatives. There is a right way and a wrong way – that's all. Mind you, I'm not always right, don't think that by any means. I've miscalculated a great many things. Very often you imagine certain things and then the audience tells you differently. You must never underestimate the audience. The audience is, after all, always right. Sometimes they react the way you don't want them to and sometimes there are a lot of kids in the house and they laugh at the wrong place. But the audience is always right. You must not be hysterical, though; you must interpret their reactions calmly and correctly. You must know cause and effect. If you had a bad laugh in the fourth reel that doesn't mean the line is bad. It simply means that what preceded, what came before the line, is all off . . . that the preparation for the line is wrong. You must be detached and look at your children from a distance . . . you must be patient and loving.

When you are filming are you often thinking of audience reactions?

No, not at all. I'm thinking of myself . . . just me and what I like. I'm not trying to guess what the audience does.

You're not trying to gauge a certain type of public then? Filming for a particular type of audience?

No. That is the kiss of death. You must please yourself. You must profoundly please yourself hoping that the audience will like it as well. If you're trying to outguess the audience or trying to be 'popular' only one sort of product can come out: a synthetic one – and it's not really you. It's false.

Of all your pictures which one did you most enjoy filming? It certainly wasn't The Chapman Report. . . .

No, it wasn't that one! I must tell you that when I work the atmosphere has to be happy, cheerful . . . amusing and funny. That doesn't mean that there aren't all sorts of *crises*, but I will not put up with strain – I can't think, I'm distracted. And I will not have unpleasant

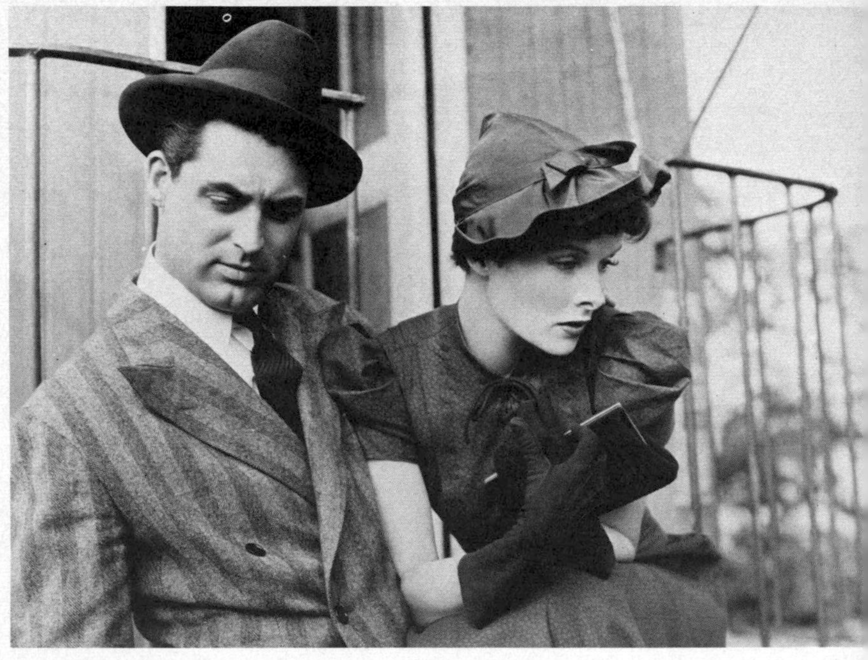

Sylvia Scarlett: Cary Grant. Katharine Hepburn

pressures on the set. Unless I'm sympathetic with people I cannot function. All the pictures I've done have been joyous experiences . . . there must be this happiness while we work – it must be enjoyable. This doesn't necessarily mean that the picture will be good, though. As a matter of fact, one film where every day was Christmas on the set and where presents were exchanged right and left was a complete disaster: *Sylvia Scarlett*.

Here was a picture where Cary Grant first felt an audience liked him. Up to then he had been a rather handsome, rather wooden leading man . . . somewhat inexperienced, too. But suddenly during the shooting he felt all his talents coming into being – maybe because it was the first part which really suited his background. He suddenly burst into bloom. Quite a blooming – it produced a wonderful performance.

It is an interesting moment when people come into their own. Now take Joan Fontaine, for instance. I always thought she was a talented girl and one day I requested to test her out in a few scenes. We began working together and she was completely petrified – couldn't move. The test was still interesting, though, and when it came time to do 'he Women I said, 'Let's get that girl, she's very pretty and she'll be ood for the part of the young wife.' Up to that point she had been t R.K.O. playing not too interesting leading women and she wasn't errribly good, especially in a picture she did with Fred Astaire.

There is a scene in *The Women* where she is in Reno with a lot of ther women waiting to get a divorce. Suddenly her husband calls her, here is a long conversation and she realizes that she is still in love with im. Joan did the scene, talking on the phone, and all at once every-hing fell into place. All the things she ever dreamed of happening to er as an actress, actually happened. She did this scene with the most remendous force and feeling. It was a thrilling moment when she ealized that she was an actress and after the take she looked at me and aid, 'I really am an actress.' She had been acting for four years and ot very successfully. Suddenly there was this breakthrough. It was a hrilling moment.

I try to make every picture the best. It's the only way to work. There nust be a climate of amiability and fun and excitement. Every picture do is the first one I've ever done . . . and it's the last. Making a picture enormously important to me and the experience is a joyous one.

Are you ever a little worried about starting a film – scared on the first ay of shooting?

Yes, the older you get the more scared you get. You see, the older nd wiser you are the better you see the pitfalls. The first three or four ays on the set I'm rather shaky but I plunge into my work just the ame. On those shaky first days people look at me and say: 'So, you're oing to start all over again?' I reply 'Yes . . . yes. . . .' I'm not absolutely onfident but my nerves get better. Well, everyone's nervous at first I uppose.

Do you take extra precautions on your first day of shooting – over overing shots, for example?

Sometimes yes, sometimes no. I do take the precaution of usually tarting out with scenes that aren't too complicated so I can break hings in slowly. As a matter of fact, I started *My Fair Lady* two days arlier than planned – we did all sorts of experimenting with the rain cenes to help the crew limber up, to help me break myself in. When e started with the principals a few days later we were all over our tters.

I wonder if we could take a scene from one of your pictures and discuss inside and out; how it was conceived, put together, filmed, edited and o on.

All right. You pick one.

A Star is Born: James Mason

What about the 'Somewhere There's a Someone' number from Sta Is Born *– where Judy Garland improvises a whole musical-comed production number in her front room?*

That's not quite fair because it's a musical number. They are alway so well planned out ahead of time – and most of the work there wa done by the choreographer.

Towards the end of Star Is Born, *perhaps. James Mason is in bed an Garland is out on the porch facing the ocean with Charles Bickforc Mason hears that his wife is planning to give up her career and spend th rest of her life nursing him. He cries – the camera stays on him for som time sobbing in bed. When Bickford has gone he tells his wife to make sandwich for him while he goes down to the ocean for a swim – she sing in the kitchen while he walks into the water . . . but maybe I should le you choose a scene yourself.*

I liked that scene, too. But it didn't require anything special . . . all happened so naturally. Moss Hart wrote it and I believe it was ve moving . . . mainly because of James Mason. He is a complete acto He is a man who has the greatest discretion . . . rather reserved b

'inner at Eight: John Barrymore

ature . . . a mysterious creature. To see that man break down was ery moving. But all the credit for that goes to James. He did it all imself. What I did was to let him do it and let it go on and on – let it un for a long time, let the camera stay on him for an eternity. He ecame so involved that he couldn't stop . . . and I let him do what e felt.

Let me think . . . what scene can I tell you about which required a ind of conception or a kind of direction. It's hard. There are so many f them. . . .

Maybe something from The Philadelphia Story*?*

Perhaps . . . no, no. Here is a scene. In a picture I did a long time ago alled *Dinner at Eight* which was taken from a stage play. Jack 'arrymore gave an extraordinary performance as an untalented, ourth-rate actor. He did it with the greatest subtlety. If you remember e was in his hotel room talking on the phone. This society woman 'as asking him to come to dinner and he was saying: 'Yes, I'd love to ome.' Well, Jack asked me if he could put something in and I told im he could do whatever he liked. So he added something to the line and it came out: 'Yes, I'd love to come, dear lady.' This little additio painted the whole character: a rather cheapish actor, slightly old fashioned. He created all sorts of wonderful *nuances* that way.

He always spoke in a rather actorish way in the film but when th bell hop would come in he tried to be tough, always in this rather over elegant voice: 'I gotta have a drink, see?'

He was on the skids but always hoped there was a part somewher for him. Finally, when all his plans fell through and he learned that th part he hoped to get had been given to an English actor he cried out 'English, English . . . I can be as English as anybody!!' Remember that

There was something he did with enormous wit. Still trying t convince those around him that he would play anything he declared 'Ibsen. I can play Ibsen.' Then he leaned up against the mantelpiec and proceeded to do a scene from Ibsen – a scene which never existe and which he invented all the way. It was all so obvious – he had neve heard of Ibsen. 'Mother, mother dear, give me the sun . . .' he went on not quite knowing what the hell he was saying. But he did it all wit the greatest truth.

In the scene where he was going to kill himself one had to feel tha he wanted to die beautifully, like Greta Garbo. We started the scene he crossed the room to plug up the chimney and turn on the gas . . and I said to him: 'Jack, he should not even be able to commit suicide He has always bungled everything and now some awful indignit should happen to him.' Then Jack walked across the room again . . right in the middle of the carpet was a stool and he tripped on i went spilling all over the floor – an awful middle-aged, ungracefu sprawl which was so sad and so marvellous in the picture. Even i arranging his death he blundered – the touch was just right. S unconventional.

. . . Mrs Patrick Campbell once made an exit and later when sh referred to it she said: 'I walked through a chair.' Well, Jack did tha The character he was playing thought he should die in as romantic way as possible – imagining all sorts of dramatic things as he turne the gas on. I thought this awful kind of note right in the middle of it a was quite good. It was so pathetic that way.

Did something 'just happen' like that while you were filming Th Chapman Report*?*

The Chapman Report . . . let me think.

What about the scene in the doctor's office where he is questionin Claire Bloom? Tension builds up in her to such a point that at last sh looks behind the screen which has been shielding her interrogator.

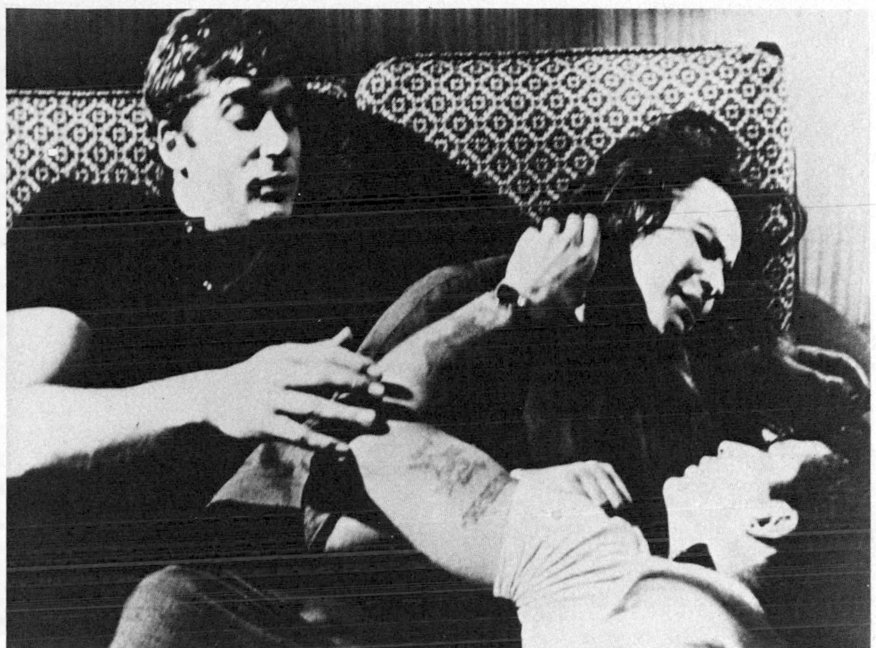

The Chapman Report: the rape scene

That was a very simple scene . . . all done in one take, by the way. We did it all in one take.

It was just a simple office – but remarkably well lighted. The colours were beautiful.

That is largely due to a good cameraman, Harold Lipstein, who was very influenced by George Hoyningen-Huene and Gene Allen.

In that scene there is a whole exposé, a whole gamut of human feelings . . . a complete human experience: defiance, lying, defences breaking down. It is a whole long betrayal.

What about the scene where Claire Bloom, in final degradation, comes to the room where the men are playing cards?

That was rather moving . . . she came in coyly, slowly, but very distinguished, and he was awful to her.

She was distinguished but she couldn't control herself.

This was very interesting. I'll tell you what we did there. The problem was to show all these men raping her. I thought it would be interesting to start it off as a game . . . the men playing around with her, laughing with her and at her, but all the time being terribly disrespectful. It all started out as a joke with the men pushing her from one place to another . . . then they did, in fact, rape her. Then the fascinating thing is that she responded to it – she was horrified but she responded to it. A fast series of cuts of pushing, shoving, grabbing, falling, grasping, arms, legs . . . the men holding her down.

In the released version we never saw any of this – just the very beginning where she is shoved down. Was this scene shown in its entirety at the San Francisco preview?

Yes, and the audience thought it was marvellous. It was very effective: the men putting their hands on her brutally, jumping on top of her . . . she got a big kick out of being indignant. And in *our* scenario, not the Zanuck final cut, she left the men, was driven away . . . went right home and killed herself. When all those people got through with it, it didn't make sense any more. I particularly liked the scene where she came into the room, her bedroom, locked the door behind her, took the bottle of pills and killed herself.

The scene with the men was of an extraordinary violence. They manhandled her, climbed on top of her and laughed. Her head moved from side to side . . . the men's gestures . . . her movements . . . a marvellous scene cut out by Zanuck. It was a long thing to shoot and we did many, many takes. The actors did it all with the greatest of delicacy. Claire was pushed around in the most violent way – her dress was ripped and torn. An agonizing experience . . . a big, heavy fellow lying on top of her . . . but the actors did it all with such delicacy, the greatest gallantry.

This was the first time you worked with Claire Bloom?

Yes, it was, and she was marvellous to work with. She's a most accomplished actress. She's played all the great parts and can do almost anything.

I asked her in one scene – where she was drunk in her bedroom – to remove her blouse. She moved across the room, slowly, like a cat . . . you saw her breasts. But all that was cut out, completely sliced to bits. Had we been able to make this picture say, in France, it would have remained intact . . . and made a sensation. As it was, we were the victims of stupid censorship, lack of courage and lack of taste. As I conceived it *and filmed it* the picture would have gone over. It would have been a sensation.

Now that you are producing your own pictures do you think you would ever come to France to do one – to be at complete liberty and to escape just such restrictions?

It depends. It depends on the kind of picture . . . it's not an impossibility. In any case, on the next film I do I don't plan to pull any punches – there is only one way to do it and next time it will be done that way.

This isn't the first time censorship has hacked away. There were scenes in *Bhowani Junction* where Ava Gardner is taking a shower . . . where she uses her lover's toothbrush and washes her mouth out with whisky. You know the scene in *Les Amants* where the man is making love to Jeanne Moreau . . . he is on her and then all of a sudden his head disappears and the camera remains on her face, her ecstasy. I did exactly the same thing in *Bhowani Junction* with Ava and Bill Travers . . . years before Louis Malle. But it all went on to the cutting-room floor.

All those things are very interesting to do, if you're allowed to do them. I sincerely believe that *The Chapman Report* had no vulgarity whatever, but after they re-arranged things . . . all the time you felt that Claire Bloom was a rather noble creature doing ignoble things. That was very important.

It was supposed to be a picture about sex, but after the cuts one hardly knew what the basic idea behind the whole thing was.

Disgraceful thing – just as well to forget it.

But we're getting away from your question about how I work. I haven't answered that very satisfactorily.

Do you work a lot with your writers?

Yes, I do. But I don't write myself.

You know, I didn't realize until I saw *The Ten Commandments* just what De Mille's strength was. A long time ago I thought what he did was a big joke, just preposterous, and I couldn't understand why the audience went for it in such a big way. There were always all sorts of orgies with belly dancers, veils and all the trappings. The eroticism was a joke. Then I saw *The Ten Commandments* . . . it was preposterous from the word go but I suddenly saw something new there, something which had escaped me before: the story-telling was wonderful. The way that man could tell a story was fascinating – you were riveted to your seat. That's exactly what he was: a great, great story-teller. It was often ridiculous with all those excesses and froth but the man did *tell a story*. That was De Mille's great talent and the secret behind his popular success.

When everything is ready for shooting, the text written, preliminary rehearsals done, do you ever come on to the set and at the last minute change something . . . at the last minute decide to take out fifteen lines, remove a big chair from the living-room, a lamp here, a pillow there?

On the set of *A Star Is Born*: 'The Man that Got Away'

Maybe I will the day before – very rarely just before the cameras roll. I try to think everything out ahead of time. I feel my way around a long time ahead to see how things can be managed. For example, in *My Fair Lady* everything was planned ahead – you have to do that for big super-spectacles.

In the Cahiers du Cinéma *interview a few years back, you talked a little bit about how you conceive the framing of shots. You cited several examples from* A Star Is Born – *which was the first true CinemaScope film, conceived expressly for the wide screen.*

On this subject I should tell you that I have working with me one of the most talented art directors in the world: Gene Allen. He has been the greatest help to me and has worked on all the pictures since *A Star Is Born*. And then there's George Hoyningen-Huene who is my colour consultant – he was, as you know, a great photographer. So you see, it's not all me – these men are responsible to a great degree.

You did many original things in framing shots in this picture. For instance, when Charles Bickford comes to console Judy Garland in her dressing-room. During that conversation you see their heads cut off on opposite sides of the screen. Just their profiles are visible with this great empty space in between.

Well . . . I don't remember that. Someplace else, though, we pushed all the action to one side and one-third . . . two-thirds of the screen was blank.

You realize, of course, that CinemaScope is the most unfortunate shape.

You don't like working in CinemaScope?

No. No. It's the most terrible shape. The old shape was the best. The old square. 70 mm. is much better. CinemaScope is such an unfortunate shape.

You certainly did some very beautiful things with it.

The problem is, you can't get any height in the thing. That makes it very difficult. All I did with my Scope pictures . . . all we did . . . was simply refuse to buckle under to the things they said you can't do. The technical people said that everything had to be played on the same plane – if someone were too much up-stage they would be out of focus. I paid no attention to that.

You said in the Cahiers *interview that for certain framings you were inspired by sections of David's* Sacre de Napoléon *reproduced in a book.*

Yes, I was. You're used to seeing the whole of a thing – then suddenly you see a section, arbitrarily, not composed. Just a section of something cut off. In the David painting you see a head to one side, bits of other heads cut off here and there when the detail is reproduced in the art book. And I thought why not do that in a movie? We made use of this especially when Judy Garland sang 'The Man That Got Away'. In the little night club after hours the camera followed her always in front . . . sometimes she went to the side and almost disappeared out of the frame . . . she was rarely right in the middle. It was all done in one long take, the whole musical number.

You often emphasize 'simplicity' in your pictures – colour, movement . . . and the one take. Do you especially like these no-cut sequences? Do you try to get them in whenever possible?

I do it whenever I can, for you get a very complete sort of result. I did it with Judy Garland because she could sustain it. It isn't easy for an actor or actress to carry a long take – you have to be strong.

In a picture called *Adam's Rib* we did almost a reel – that's about nine hundred feet . . . no, more than nine hundred feet – with no cuts. It was a scene with Katharine Hepburn in the house of detention, a women's house of detention where Judy Holliday was being interviewed by the lawyer Katharine Hepburn. It was an extremely well written sequence with Hepburn facing away from the camera for the whole thing. She had her back to the camera almost the whole time but that had a meaning: she indicated to the audience that they should look at Judy Holliday. We did that whole thing without a cut.

These long shots, prolonged sequences . . . they just happen when the scene is right. It just happens.

I notice in most of your musical numbers that there are very few cuts.

Really?

For instance in Les Girls *where the girls do their first dance number – not the 'Ladies in Waiting' but the first one. It was extremely simple – only a few cuts which were hardly perceptible.*

I don't really remember. I hate to say this, but the reason a lot of this comes out the way it does is because I always set up at least two cameras for the musical numbers. You do it with an 'A' camera and some supplementary ones just to see what happens. When it's all over you see that the 'B' camera, the one you had there for fun, is the really interesting one. It turns out to be the most fascinating. It's not always in perfect focus, it's not in perfect composition but it's very exciting, very dramatic. Sometimes you plan a scene for a series of close-ups, you know that is the only way to do it – then when the 'B' camera result comes up you realize that you were all wrong. You say to hell with the close-ups and decide to keep the long-shots. But you usually realize that when the picture is all done.

Of the 'before and after' stages of film making – scenario, cutting – which do you prefer? Do you like to monkey around with a moviola?

Not so much the moviola . . . but I'm fascinated with what can be done with cutting. For example, in this wretched *Chapman Report*, I never cut to the interrogator in the interviews with the woman. You never saw the doctor asking questions – just the woman, her facial expressions, her movements, her reactions. You were on her the entire time. It was very interesting because you just heard the man's voice off and caught the woman's reaction.

So you're not like Hitchcock then who feels that once the scenario and dialogue are written the film is all wrapped up – that the actual filming is mere mechanics.

Well, Hitchcock is an absolute master. An absolute master. And what you say is very much his style. He's a master of well thought out effects. But between you and me I'm not quite sure that he is telling the complete truth. He must improvise with performances sometimes. There was a picture of his called *Suspicion* where Joan Fontaine gave the most extraordinary performance. Now, I can't believe that that was all mechanical – all planned out ahead of time. Very often it is, especially in his case . . . but not always. He is hiding things from you; he doesn't say how he works, how he achieves effects – easier to say it was all planned in the script and the rest is mechanics.

Sometimes the actor feels that he is being directed by someone with taste who will automatically bring out the best in them . . . who will not have to tell them a great deal. The actor just *feels* the director's presence, his will, what he wants. I don't know what Hitchcock says . . . all I know is that he is an absolute master. I like Hitchcock. I think he's a very original man, a great man . . . very talented. He's left his mark. The very word 'Hitchcock' means 'mystery story' – it's become synonymous with 'suspense'. His name has become a word with a rich meaning.

So has yours.

No. Not quite . . . no, no.

Maybe not entirely in America, but certainly here in Europe.

Maybe I'll come here and spend my declining days then. And they're fast approaching.

I'm very touched at the *real* interest in my films here.

You knew, of course, that the Cinémathèque Française organized a 'hommage' to you last summer and over a three-week period showed practically all your films?

I had heard something about that. There was a man in New York last year who said: 'We should have a George Cukor festival,' but he was just making a joke. I was going to answer him with a joke, answer his snide remark . . . but I thought, what the hell!

Yes, I did hear something about the Cinémathèque. It's a film library, isn't it?

Yes, and every day they have showings of six different films.

Howard Hawks. He's one of the sacred cows, isn't he?

And Hitchcock, too . . . with the Cahiers *crowd.*

Well, they should admire him. They certainly should. They like Nicholas Ray, too. He's pretty hot stuff.

How do you have all this inside dope on film tastes in France?

Because I read *Cahiers du Cinéma*. Sometimes I'm very amused at reading these very nice articles about my work . . . and then I read what they think of other gentlemen and I think. . . . Well, I don't know what to think. I'm not so sure, then, that their judgment is all that. . . .

I'd like to ask you two very superficial questions.

And I'll give you two very superficial answers.

This is the 'Aurore-type' question: What are your favourite pictures, Mr Cukor? [Cukor was interviewed the day before by a reporter from the Paris daily, Aurore. *Consequently, he now refers to all chit-chatty-type questions as* Aurorish.*]*

I really haven't any. I have favourite pictures which other people have made, though.

What are they?

I loved a picture called *Lady With A Little Dog*. It was Russian. A most ravishing, marvellous film.

It's a very peculiar thing to ask. There are so many pictures which I have enjoyed but I have no particular favourite – of my own.

You cannot look back. When you reach my age you must look forward. You can't say: This was awfully nice, and I did this and that and it was pretty good. . . .

There must be some which you like for certain reasons. Maybe Camille*?*

Well, I cherish that one because it was a success.

I'll tell you something very interesting about that film. A bit of Aurore talk. . . . When *Camille* was previewed it was shown with two other Metro pictures the same evening. The picture was dismissed. Garbo was dismissed – the whole thing was dismissed as no good. I was given a rather bad notice – and it was all because I didn't want to advertise in a trade paper. They cut the hell out of me and the film because I did not wish to advertise. You know the type of advertising I mean – your name in a trade paper, put there regularly and heavily paid for. The treatment of *Camille* had the most extraordinary effect on me. From then on, I said about advertising: 'finita!' They heckle you about advertising and it's always embarrassed me to advertise because when I was very young, before I ever went into 'show biz', the only advertising you got was with vaudeville acts. Someone would come out on the stage and say: 'At liberty . . .' and then sell the bill of goods. And that sticks in my craw as something terribly cheap about the whole thing.

So now when they come to me and say: 'Would you advertise?' I reply: 'Well, let me see the review first.' I have not advertised my name in a trade paper since 1936. And nothing will get me to do it. When President Wilson died everyone put their name in the papers . . . surrounded by a black band. Advertising just the same. I never do it. Never! Not in the *Reporter*, *Variety*, *The Year Book*. . . .

I'd like to ask you a few questions about your cameramen, the directors of photography, as they say over here.

Why haven't you used Daniels or Ruttenberg lately?

Those men were under contract to M.G.M. And some of them . . . not Ruttenberg . . . are great stars in their own right and refuse to listen, refuse to be influenced. Now that I've worked with Gene Allen and Hoyningen-Huene I've become spoiled – I must have cameramen who will listen. Lipstein is very good and so is a man called Danny Fapp who did *Let's Make Love*, the Marilyn Monroe picture. He is a wonderful technician who knows a great deal and he will listen. With him you don't have all the boring things that cameramen do – you put your foot down and you don't have it.

For example, we started out with Harry Stradling, who is, by the way, a very talented man. I said to him, 'Harry, these sets are very well painted, the colours are perfect as they are and we don't want any more colour of any kind . . . no filters!' He's rather tough and said that he wouldn't put any colour in. Well, when I saw the rushes I discovered that he had snuck a little colour in – some little nuances way in the back. So I said to him again, 'No colour, Harry. No colour!' He finally got the idea that I meant business. The set was beautiful and there was no need to jazz it up with any more colour.

What picture was this?

My Fair Lady. But he was very good about this finally. Cameramen get into all kinds of habits and one has to watch them very carefully. It's best to have somcone with an open mind who won't put in all sorts of boring shadows and things like that. You have to give these men their head because they're artists – you have to stimulate them, not let them fall back on habits.

In the old Metro days, whom did you like best to work with, Daniels or Ruttenberg?

I only did black and white pictures with them. I don't know. I like them both.

What is the difference between the two men?

I think Daniels was a much more original and daring innovator. Now he plays it safe . . . what is he doing now . . . a great photographer of Lollobrigida, I think.

We were going to do *Lady L* . . . based on the novel of Romain Gary, and Lollobrigida had the lead. We were doing make-up tests and I said to her, 'Gina, you can't have the Cinecitta look . . . all that heavy orange crust on your face.' 'My eyes,' she replied. And all the time Daniels was trying to tell me that he was going to put some colour in the thing, change the colour of her face.

I tried to tell them that this was a period picture, that the women had white skin and pink cheeks and did not have any god-damned Italian sunburn on! Well, Lollobrigida looked like the rice fields . . . or whatever the hell. And Daniels was with her a little bit. I got out of patience with him a little bit. He never used to be that way – I thought he was more independent. I do not like people who ingratiate themselves with the stars.

There used to be a wonderful cameraman who died . . . Frank Planer. . . .

He started to do the Marilyn Monroe picture and years ago he did *Holiday*. He was *very* modern, very sensitive. He didn't use key lights and things like that. He was simple and direct and did the most marvellous things.

You did some pictures with Robert Planck as cameraman, didn't you?

Yes. He's dead now. . . . I liked him very much. We did a picture together with Joan Crawford called *A Woman's Face*.

I particularly liked the snow scene at the end.

That was all done by the second unit, you know. It was brilliantly photographed and put together – technically. Technically . . . that was the whole thing. It was pure fabrication. There wasn't really snow, there wasn't really a waterfall, there wasn't really an aerial railroad. It was all achieved with such dazzling tricks, marvellous technique.

What do you think of Milton Krasner?

I think Krasner is very good. I did *A Double Life* and *The Model and the Marriage Broker* with him. He's worked a lot with Minnelli, I think. I'm not so sure that I like his colour work that much, though.

But Surtees . . . Robert Surtees . . . is a master. He is very easily stimulated. He did *Les Girls*.

The colour in that was superb.

That is not Surtees. That is Huene.

Surtces is so sensitive. You give him pictures of things and say, 'Look at this painting. Isn't it great!' And he'll reply, 'I can't wait to get to the studio tomorrow morning and try that.' You have to stimulate these people and he was stimulated – he loved it, having new ideas.

What about Frederick Young with whom you did Bhowani Junction *and* Edward, My Son*?*

Freddy Young? I think he's a very, very talented man.

Did you see Lawrence Of Arabia*? What did you think of the photography?*

I thought it was a wonderful picture, a wonderful picture . . . but I don't think it was a satisfying picture. You mustn't say this to anyone, but I think there was a sort of *folie de grandeur* in *Lawrence*. You know, they all took themselves so frightfully serious and it was much too long . . . and too grandiose. I think the real *core* of the story escaped them. After I came out I really couldn't say what they were trying to tell me. The *story* wasn't there. Mind you, he was a curious creature, Lawrence, but I didn't know what their point was. It was lost in all those surging masses. It was just too much. That's what happens when someone has a hit. The next time it has to be bigger and better. They get terrified and forget tradition.

Young is a very talented man . . . not easily influenced, though. He is rather nervous and he makes me a little nervous although I like him very much.

Can you tell me a little bit about Hoyningen-Huene? Who is he? How did he start working with you?

He is half-Russian, half-American. A man who has enormous taste about everything . . . a photographer for *Vogue*, *Harper's Bazaar*, and he did some wonderful books on Greece, Palmyra and Baalbec. The first picture I did with him was *A Star Is Born* and he influenced everything.

How does he work – what is his function on one of your pictures?

He works on the overall design of the picture and is there when it's being photographed. He knows everything about film and influences so many things . . . from sets to colour effects, to costumes . . . he works in close collaboration with Gene Allen.

While we were preparing *Lady L* . . . they were assisted by Leslie Blanche (Mrs Romain Gary) and Orry Kelly was doing the clothes. The combination was thrilling. The sets were ravishing. It would have been one of the most extraordinary films – what they produced was unbelievable. From no other people could you have gotten such beautiful results.

George works on the sets, the general design, the use of colour . . . he does all that. He selects every bit of material. For example, if we need a grey on a wall or on a chair, anywhere, he looks it over, scrutinizes it, and if it's the wrong grey, too blue perhaps, he changes it. He edits colour and nothing escapes him.

For example, he does the most unconventional things. We were doing a scene in *Les Girls*, a London exterior, and he said, 'The whole thing should be this one colour – the dresses, the room later on, the exterior walls, the sidewalk, the sky, the fences.' Everything was the colour of clay and I said, 'Isn't that going to be awfully dull and drab?' He assured me that it wouldn't. He was right and the effect was wonderful. He used this same 'uniformity of colour' in *Let's Make Love*. Everything in Yves Montand's office was beige and brown. The effect was one of great beauty.

If you notice in *Les Girls* the colour comes in 'packages'. Sometimes the girls are in red, sometimes in blue, sometimes in black. It's not a *mélange* but wonderfully edited.

In *Heller in Pink Tights* do you remember those clothes for the wild west productions of *Mazeppa* and *La Belle Hélène* with Sophia Loren, Anthony Quinn and their company? George went down into the basement of the studio, to the wardrobe storage place where nobody ever goes, and he came back with old costumes of the crusades, the Revolution . . . all sorts of incorrect things falling apart and he put them all together. It was so real on the screen, all the actors in the far west with this incredible *mélange*.

Heller in Pink Tights: Sophia Loren, Anthony Quinn

The colour in the cabaret-saloon was wonderful . . . all deep red, rich green. . . .

Yes . . . that was Gene Allen there. Wasn't that wonderful the colour of the walls – intense red. Do you remember where she was in black and then when she was all in white and the men were all in black . . . she wanders through the saloon, exploring it, opening windows, sticking her head through, framing herself by the red walls . . . It was clean and bold.

In *Les Girls* one girl wore one colour all the way through and another wore another colour.

Take the office scene in *The Chapman Report*. Gene Allen and Hoyningen-Huene influenced the lighting. It was logical lighting. The outside was lighter than the inside. There were none of the clichés that you usually have. I insist that lighting be logical – light should be where it would normally be in a real setting. You see, look over there at the window. It's dark inside this room and when you look in the direction of the window the light source is all burnt up. You don't tone down outside light just to get artificial balance. The sky is not blue all the time – sometimes it's grey. It could be any colour. Cameramen, of necessity, put lights in the wrong places . . . to be pretty. They jazz things up with key lights that are very old-fashioned: it's photography of the past; a slight shadow on the eye, the eyelash throwing a shadow. It's a lot of work watching out for all these things, establishing the composition, establishing the position of the camera.

What is Gene Allen's role?

Gene Allen is a very talented set designer – an art director who does everything. He also writes and did some of the scenes in *The Chapman Report*. He will be a brilliant producer some day. He started out as a detective because his father was a police captain. On his vacations he worked in the studio as a print boy and taught art. When I first met him he was a sketch artist and I found him very talented – so I hired him. He writes scenarios and hopes to be a producer or maybe even a director.

He did some wonderful sets for *A Star Is Born* and for *My Fair Lady*. Although the sets were supposed to be done in collaboration with Cecil Beaton, he, in fact, did most of the work while Beaton concentrated on the clothes.

How did you like working with Beaton for the first time?

I don't like Beaton. He was the only sour note in the whole picture.

But he certainly brought his great talent to the service of the picture.

Yes, he did. He's enormously clever. He knows everything there is to know about Edwardian costumes but I dislike him.

Did Hoyningen-Huene work on My Fair Lady*?*

No. Beaton was engaged before I had anything to do with the picture.

How is My Fair Lady *different from your other pictures – have you tried anything new or different here?*

No, it is not different from the other films . . . no great revolution in style, that is. I thought that *My Fair Lady* was such a perfect work . . . the combination of Shaw and music . . . a minor masterpiece. All I could do was bring it to the screen with as much style and truth as I could. And that's what I did.

From the stills I have seen, the sets appear to be very stylized. This appears to be a little innovation because in your other pictures sets are usually so real right down to the little details.

This is somewhat out of necessity. We couldn't do Ascot realistically. Everything is in its own world – Covent Garden is a reproduction of Covent Garden. We've worked for a poetic stylization.

I'll tell you something about the conception. When Audrey sings 'Wouldn't It Be Loverly' she dances with people of seventy and eighty who had never appeared on the screen before. We went all over the place to find them. When Audrey dances with them it is fresh and charming. Then when you go to Wimpole Street it isn't really Wimpole Street. Of course, you can't sing on a real Wimpole Street so we put together a composite of things. Ascot is probably the most stylized, though.

This is the first time I've worked in 70 mm. and also for the first time with a six-track sound system.

After the unpleasant experience with one producer on the previous picture, how did you get along with Jack Warner?

Jack Warner? He's tough but he's a showman. Quite a remarkable showman, I might add. He's very intelligent. This picture is sort of the apotheosis of his career and he did everything. He is a perfect gentleman. Everything depended on him and he behaved wonderfully . . . generously and courageously.

I think *My Fair Lady* is a charming picture. If you liked the play . . . it is exactly like it, but it's a movie. Audrey plays with a great deal of power in it. She's a hard worker . . . extremely intelligent, inventive, modest . . . and funny. To work with her you wouldn't think she was this great star. She's tactful . . . the most endearing creature in the world. Rex Harrison is magnificent, too. He gives a great performance, just as he did on the stage.

One has the impression that you do quite a bit of documenting before starting a picture. You certainly did for My Fair Lady, *in any case.*

Yes, the ground work must be well gone over. You must be familiar with the climate of your subject down to the smallest details. When I am going to do a picture on New York I go to New York and look all around, all around. I look at locales with different eyes because when you know you are going to do a film you see things altogether differently, with different eyes. I delve into the texture of life and reality.

For instance, when we were preparing *The Actress* we went to see an old house that served as a model for the one in the film. It was a wonderful house and had a kitchen with six doors. We used that kitchen . . . not *exactly* the same way, but almost. Reality must be observed then transmuted. If I were going to film this hotel room I would begin to see it with new eyes. I would look all around, see that newspaper over there, those books. Mind you, I couldn't film it just as it is – I would make notes in my mind about the casual bits of reality and then re-create the whole thing.

What about your historical pictures . . . how do you research and 'observe reality' here?

I look at photographs of the time, paintings, read books, look at old engravings. For one picture I looked at an old photograph of my grandfather . . . no, it was a picture which my grandfather had given me of the Civil War. I am very influenced by paintings and old photographs.

When we were preparing *Lady L* . . . I looked at numerous paintings by Boldini, Sargent. I also looked at portraits by Van Dongen . . . to get a smell of the period.

When I filmed *David Copperfield* I went to the actual places where the action was to take place. The slightest things gave me ideas.

In *My Fair Lady* there is a scene where Eliza's father sings 'With a Little Bit of Luck'. He leaves a bar and, slightly drunk, wanders along in some trenches with a group of workmen. I was inspired to do this because I had once seen a painting of the period representing some workmen.

It was fun working with all the technical phonetic inventions. We had a technical adviser come over from U.C.L.A. and he brought all sorts of period phonetic machines. For instance, for the breathing, they used a candle on the stage but we found a marvellous contraption

. . . it was a complicated thing with all sorts of mirrors that turned and revolved and indicated if your breathing was right or not.

Mrs Higgins was an *art nouveau*, intellectual sort of lady so we dressed her all in modern style. There was considerable research done for this picture over a long period of time.

What sort of research went into Camille*?*

The same . . . I looked at many paintings of the period, many obscure ones.

One of the first shots of *Camille* is when she is walking through the glittering halls of the Opéra. There are a lot of men standing around smoking, with their hats on, top hats. There was a problem: how should Garbo walk through this group of arrogant men? She was a courtesan, had a certain reputation and couldn't walk through the crowd like a 'respectable' woman would. Garbo moved through them marvellously – she carried herself proudly, almost slipped through as if to avoid their glances. Garbo invented this. But if I had it to do all over again I would do it differently – she wouldn't 'slip' through. She would be much more proud and aloof . . . haughty.

Faulkner said when working on Hawks's Land of the Pharaohs *he had trouble with the dialogue because he had no idea how Egyptians talked. How do you solve this problem . . . how do you know how people in the mid-1800s talked?*

In the first place, Faulkner was much too practical minded. I'm not saying this in a derogatory way, but when you do dialogue you have to have a free mind, create, make things up which have the ring of truth. Faulkner found it difficult to create things which he himself had not experienced . . . in part. Right now I am planning a picture on mediums around 1874. Every century has its own flavour and colour and you have to catch that. It may not be perfectly accurate right down the line but if it manages to catch the 'flavour' that's what counts.

This is what we did for *Les Girls*. The set was not an exact slice of reality but a combination of things. We came to Paris and climbed up six and seven flights of stairs and took stills of this room and that room. The set was a composite of all sorts of elements. It was filmed in Hollywood and done in CinemaScope proportion. The scenes, the sets, had to be specially designed for the CinemaScope proportion.

There was a scene where the girls are eating. Usually food in a scene is left to the last minute to the property man who rushes off to the studio commissary to get a few pieces of ham, some bread . . . and spreads them all over the table. But in *Les Girls* we had the most wonderful, real French food . . . down to the smallest details. We even looked at Cézanne's still lifes . . . the great Impressionist. On the table were wine and cheeses and with the girls all around it was pure Cézanne. There was quite a bit of loving thought put into it and it paid off – scenes must be done this way, with no slap-dash about them. I do them with a great deal of affection and detail.

It seems to me, that there is always a certain logic in the way you put musical numbers together . . . the way you introduce music and singing into the dramatic action. Songs never seem to come at unnatural places – the placement of the 'number' is much less 'stylized' than in Minnelli's musicals. In A Star Is Born, *for instance, one doesn't stop and say: Now the music starts and the dialogue stops. One flows into the other in a most natural way.*

I am not a musical-comedy director, you know. I just don't have the experience. I am not very skilful about putting songs in, I suppose. It has to be *natural*; I can't seem to get them in really clever spots. The screen is terribly logical – and once you establish your logic, anything can be fitted into it, anything can happen. Like all those prisoners singing in René Clair's *A Nous la Liberté*. The screen is so logical . . . I don't know enough about music to put songs in more cleverly, more skilfully.

It's important not to have any real rules, solid do's and don't's. Nothing should be sung arbitrarily . . . this idea has always stuck in my craw. We started doing the Rex Harrison number, 'Why Can't the English', but somehow the thing was robbed of all its vitality. We tried it every way to make it work but to no avail. Finally Rex got mad and started singing in indignation. That worked! It was perfect.

I must be very logical about music. I don't have the assurance of Donen or Minnelli. They are born musical directors.

There's one big thing to keep in mind. . . . Garson Kanin once said apropos one of his plays which he was just opening, 'The audience will not stand for any bullshit.' That is true . . . the audience is right and they will not take any bullshit.

What stage musical have you enjoyed?

I adored *How To Succeed in Business Without Really Trying*. It has tremendous style and wit.

Minnelli's Gigi*?*

I really didn't care for it too much. It was trying to be too typically French – ooh la la, and all that.

What about your association with Lubitsch on One Hour With You*?*

Lubitsch was the producer but he didn't have time to shoot the picture. He was an extremely busy man. I did the shooting and Lubitsch didn't like what I did. It was an awkward time of my life. . . . I sued Paramount because they wanted to take my name off the picture. I went right into the head office and said: 'All right, give me 100,000 dollars!' Well, maybe it wasn't that much but it was quite a bit. At that time David Selznick had gone to R.K.O. and wanted me to come over there with him. Paramount wouldn't let me go – so I agreed to drop my law suit if they would release me. They did and that's how I left.

When I came to Hollywood it was just at the time when talkies were coming in. Everyone thought I was a New York sophisticate. They immediately typed me. For a while I did nothing but costume pictures . . . then this kind, then that. . . .

While we're on the subject of musicals, can we talk a little about A Star Is Born*? I think it's one of the greatest musicals of all time.*

Did you see it in its entire version, the uncut one?

Many years ago, when it first came out in America. Recently I've seen the version here in France.

That's very badly cut. That's the foreign version . . . all cut and trimmed with some very important parts missing.

The big dance number towards the end, 'Somewhere There's a Someone', seems casual. Judy Garland improvises a musical production number in the living-room in front of her husband. Was that number in any way improvised?

No, not at all. It was carefully rehearsed. Very carefully rehearsed. She gave it the effect of improvisation, but it was created to give that impression . . . very carefully rehearsed. I don't know whether you saw a picture I did with Jack Lemmon and Judy Holliday called *It Should Happen to You*. They are in a bar and Jack is playing the piano. He was very happy singing and she just happened to be singing along with him and they 'just happened' to do the whole bit. Well, that was all very carefully rehearsed. Judy's such a good musician and so is he. The scene was so casual and they were singing and talking. They started out by saying, 'Let's fall in love . . .' then he started playing. You had the impression that it was evolving for the first time before your eyes . . . but it was very carefully prepared.

When you work with an actress, do you like to establish a personal or emotional rapport with her before you start working – or can you just start out cold?

You can do all sorts of preparation but nothing can be planned out perfectly ahead of time. The proof of the pudding is the eating. You know, you can make propositions, you can talk and you can establish a sort of friendly relationship. But when you're before the cameras with your actress you're sort of alone with your god. There you are. When the cameras start to purr it really happens. Up to then it's very polite and hopeful and cordial. You establish a relationship before but the real 'working relationship' doesn't happen until you're working.

I asked you this because you seem to have a way of getting under an actress's hide – of coaxing extraordinary performances from any woman.

Well, I think that most of these ladies are very practical-minded and expect you to deliver the goods. They have to feel that what you're telling them makes sense. This is very important. After you establish a rapport with them you can tell them the most devasting things. They don't care as long as they trust your judgment and have confidence in you. They don't care as long as they feel that you are watching them very sharply and sympathetically. You can say anything to them as long as you make them feel that they will eventually get it. You don't treat them like hopeless cases, you see. You can say awful things to them because you believe they will eventually get it . . . and they know that you believe.

It's a quirk of fate that you made My Fair Lady *– in a way you yourself are a Pygmalion. You seem to specialize in bringing movie 'idols' to life, or at least into 'being'. . . .*

Well, all directors do that to some extent . . . but there are so many who are not really interested in making their actors come alive before the camera. There are some wonderful directors who are not terribly interested in performances – who are much more intrigued by the picture as a whole. They will build up an effect of a door knob turning rather than concentrating on the actor's face. I think human values are more important. Human behaviour, to me, is what makes things go.

Most of your pictures have been with actresses who are big stars. What do you think of doing pictures with people who are totally unknown? Do you feel more in your element with the 'sacred beasts'?

I've done more pictures than you think with unknowns and a great many people started out with me. Let me think offhand . . . there was Angela Lansbury in *Gaslight*. Jack Lemmon . . . and Aldo Ray.

Was The Marrying Kind *his first picture?*

No, he played a taxi driver, just a bit part, the time before and then in *The Marrying Kind* he had a long, leading part. He was a constable in Crockett, California and he really didn't want to become an actor. His brother heard that they were going to do a picture up there, something about football, and Aldo went to do a test. I saw that test. We were preparing *The Marrying Kind* and Garson Kanin and Ruth Gordon had their hearts set on Sid Caesar for the lead. He turned it down . . . wasn't good enough for him.

Anyway, here was Aldo . . . in the test I saw he did something very interesting. He was sitting on the floor playing cards, just throwing them out in all directions. I thought he would be great for the part. By this time, though, the boy had gone back to Crockett – but he was still under option, so I asked the producer to bring him down for another test.

He came to Hollywood but he was too fat. I told him to lose weight and he did; in fact, he lost thirty pounds. Some incredible amount. I began making tests and we worked very hard on them. He was a natural sort of actor with enormous individuality. When we were through I sent the tests out to Ruth Gordon and Garson Kanin and they thought he was marvellous. So we signed him up.

When we began shooting the first day he froze up. I knew it was dead terror – the same thing happened to Shelley Winters on the first picture she did with me. It was the Colman film, *A Double Life*. She too made a very good test and then was absolutely frozen, didn't know what the hell she was doing and completely terrified.

Aldo was scared to death and he lost everything. After a day or two he relaxed and about the third or fourth day he did a scene with Judy Holliday – a silent scene – where he lay on the bed and did some silent acting which is very difficult to do. Judy was lost in admiration for him. . . . He has a great advantage: the way his eyes are made. The light comes into them. There are certain people who have opaque eyes which refuse to catch the light. But his eyes had a certain glow and gave quite well in the photographed result. He did this silent scene very well lying there on the bed in the same room with Judy. Then later he did comedy scenes with her and alone – very difficult ones – and there were also emotional sequences where he broke down and cried. They were brilliant.

He did his next picture with me . . . with Spencer Tracy and Katharine Hepburn. That was *Pat and Mike* and he played the role of a punchy prizefighter. Then I don't know what happened to him. I haven't seen him play for quite some time now and it's a shame for he's a very talented actor. . . .

Perhaps you could tell me something about the actual direction of your actors and actresses – do you have a technique? . . . Was there any influence from Lubitsch?

Lubitsch, you know, wrote everything out beforehand. Everything was so carefully calculated in advance. He worked night and day with his writers, supervised everything – everything was down pat, perfect. He knew exactly what was to be said and done. I'm not that rigid. In places I allow room for improvisation. I feel my way more. . . .

You can rehearse up to a certain point, but not too far. For example, Rex Harrison . . . I would not let him rehearse. During rehearsals he had a tendency to give too much of himself and there wasn't enough left for the real thing. Rehearsals are just meant for going through the mechanics of the thing. In the actual being before the camera something must be discovered; there must be an electricity there that can only come the first time something is done. Before, you just go through the motions and let yourself go when your time comes. . . . When you are before the camera things should 'happen'. Good people will vary it every time, for every take . . . make it fresh, give little changes each time. You know how some dumb actresses will say: 'I can't do it unless I believe it.' Well, there's truth in that. If you have too much rehearsal it becomes mechanical.

I never tell them what they should do. I coax, persuade, push sometimes. But it's important to let them discover reactions and feelings in the character they're playing. Everything is not perfectly laid out ahead of time and on the set I'm not a dictator. There must be a pleasant happy atmosphere.

Perhaps you could give me a few thumb-nail sketches . . . thumb-nail impressions, rather, on some of the actresses you've worked with.

Who? You name them.

Joan Crawford.

She was and is a great movie personality. You can photograph her from any angle, from any side, anywhere, under any conditions . . . she always looks good. But her real talent is the way she moves. All she has to do is walk across the room, from one side to the other, and you notice that something very special is happening. The way she carries herself, the way her arms move . . . the position of the head . . . she attracts attention simply by moving and she arrests you. She wouldn't have to open her mouth – just walk – and she would be superb. But look, she did that in the silent films, didn't she? Albert Finney has the same talent for 'moving'.

Ava Gardner.

She interferes with herself. She's extremely intelligent. A fatalistic

Camille: Greta Garbo, Robert Taylor

woman. A creature of great fascination . . . and of desperation. An extraordinary beauty. You know, she doesn't think a hell of a lot of herself as an actress. That's too bad.

In *Bhowani Junction* she did some marvellous erotic scenes, as I told you. She used his toothbrush in a very special way, brushed her teeth with whisky. Very low class and exciting. But this was all cut by the censors.

Lana Turner.

I directed her in *A Life of Her Own*. All I can remember about that one is that I hated it. It was an awful story. When we went to the first story conference, I couldn't believe my ears. It was terrible. At the beginning she was supposed to kill herself and then they wouldn't even let her do that.

In closing, maybe a few words about Garbo.

I directed her in her last picture, *Two-Faced Woman*, in 1941. We started doing it without a script and this is always dangerous. Garbo was extremely well behaved and disciplined. She made many, many requests but they were always practical and reasonable.

She had great self-possession. She requested that no one come on the set while she was filming. She had an idea, a notion of illusion that went very far and she didn't want to break it. People around shattered this illusion – and then she didn't want gawkers to see her 'unguarded' while she worked. Thought if they wanted to see her they should go to her pictures. She never saw rushes because they always fell short of what she thought she could do . . . of what she imagined. A great perfectionist . . . to the extreme.

She often had to quit working early to calm down – when she acted she put her whole self into it and it wore her down, exhausted her.

She liked to work the way I do: very sketchy rehearsals and real acting done for the first time before the cameras.

She had a talent that few actresses or actors possess. In close-ups she gave the impression, the illusion of great movement. She would move her head just a little bit and the whole screen would come alive – like a strong breeze that made itself felt. Wonderful movement. Technically, she was enormously resourceful. She always had great trust in the people she worked for – most of the time.

She knew how to act for the camera . . . for the camera.

Irving Thalberg died after the first week of shooting on *Two-Faced Woman* but saw the first rushes. He was amazed and said to me, 'She's never been so good! She is unguarded for the first time.' The picture was bad but he was right when he said that she was unguarded for the first time. She was never so fragile and unprotected. . . . It was already the end.

It was an interesting idea to have her play twin sisters but the script wasn't written – we did it as we went along and it just went bad. It was too bad for Garbo. . . .

It is hard to talk about Garbo, really, for she says everything when she appears on the screen. That is GARBO . . . and all you say is just so much chit-chat. There she is on the screen. How she achieves those effects may or may not be interesting. She is what she is; and that is a very creative actress who *thinks* about things a great deal and has a very personal way of acting.

You have to give her her head – let her do what she feels. If you remember in *Camille* when the father comes in to tell her to leave his son, she falls to the ground and puts her hand on the table. That's a very original thing to do. One must let her do these things and they happen marvellously.

Also, do you remember in *Camille* when the man made her pick up her fan – he just stood there, the Baron de Varville. When she reached down she did the most unforgettable thing. Sweeping down, like a dancer . . . Isadora Duncan . . . she swept it up – the whole motion was done without bending her knees. It was so unexpected for it is not a natural gesture. Yet, it was pure grace when she did it – just that way for some peculiar reason. [At this point Cukor rises and tries to imitate the movement.] I can't do it. Impossible. The *plastique* of her body was marvellous. She doesn't move like a ballerina acting – but like an actress acting. It is not dance but acting. This is an important point. She moves like an actress. Margot Fonteyn is an actress in this sense. There was a bit of Garbo in her performance of *La Dame aux Camélias*.

I think all you have to know about Garbo is what you see on the screen. How she achieves what she does is a mystique. . . .

In Camille *I particularly liked the scene where she wakes up for the first time in the country. Sitting up in bed with the morning light streaming in, it is as though she is re-born.*

She is primitive, in fact. She's basically like an animal. She likes the smell of the ground. . . .

George Cukor: films as director

1930: *Grumpy* (with Cyril Gardner), *The Virtuous Sin* (with Louis Gasnier), *The Royal Family of Broadway* (with Cyril Gardner)

1931: *Tarnished Lady, Girls about Town*

1932: *One Hour with You* (directed by Cukor from a plan by Lubitsch; credited to Lubitsch), *What Price Hollywood?*, *A Bill of Divorcement, Rockabye, Our Betters*

1933: *Dinner at Eight, Little Women*

1934: *David Copperfield*

1935: *Sylvia Scarlett*

1936: *Romeo and Juliet, Camille*

1938: *Holiday* (*Free to Live*), *Zaza*

1939: *Gone with the Wind* (first three weeks' shooting), *The Women*

1940: *Susan and God* (*The Gay Mrs Trexal*), *The Philadelphia Story*

1941: *A Woman's Face, Two-Faced Woman*

1942: *Her Cardboard Lover*

1943: *Keeper of the Flame, Resistance and Ohm's Law* (short for U.S. Signal Corps)

1944: *Gaslight* (*Murder in Thornton Square*), *Winged Victory*

1947: *Desire Me* (with Jack Conway), *A Double Life*

1948: *Edward, My Son*

1949: *Adam's Rib*

1950: *A Life of Her Own, Born Yesterday*

951: *The Model and the Marriage Broker*

952: *The Marrying Kind, Pat and Mike*

1953: *The Actress*

1954: *It Should Happen to You, A Star is Born*

955: *Bhowani Junction*

957: *Les Girls, Wild is the Wind*

959: *Song Without End* (completed by Cukor after Vidor's death)

960: *Heller in Pink Tights, Let's Make Love*

961: *The Chapman Report*

962: *Something's Got to Give* (abandoned on the death of Marilyn Monroe)

964: *My Fair Lady*

968: *Justine*

Rouben Mamoulian talking to Andrew Sarris, 1966

Rouben Mamoulian holds court at the Drake Hotel in New York when he is away from his home in Beverly Hills, California. Among film and stage directors, he is extraordinarily precise in his interviews. He has lectured at many universities and museums and has written such articles as 'The World's Latest Fine Art'; 'Use of Colour on the Screen'; 'Colours Are Emotions'; 'Use and Abuse of Camera Perambulation'; 'George Gershwin'; 'D.W. Griffith, Director'; 'Stage and Screen'; 'Eleanora Duse vs. Sarah Bernhardt'; 'Colour and Lighting in Films from 1946 to 1956'; 'Hollywood Needs a Laboratory'; and 'The Function of Motion Picture Criticism'. He is also the author of two books: Abigayil, Story of the Cat at the Manger *(1964) and* Shakespeare's Hamlet, A New Version *(1966).*

Rouben Mamoulian's theoretical formulations are, however, only the footnotes to a career of extraordinary innovations on stage and screen. Applause *and* City Streets *have been honoured in their time and after for helping break the sound barrier, and* Becky Sharp *was the first feature film in Technicolor, and is usually cited in any tract on the colour film. Yet this is the same man who directed such landmarks of the American theatre as* Porgy, Porgy and Bess, Marco Millions, R.U.R., Wings

Over Europe, Oklahoma!, Carousel, St Louis Woman, Lost in the Stars. *This is a man who has directed Greta Garbo, Marlene Dietrich, Helen Morgan, Irene Dunne, Sylvia Sidney, Alla Nazimova, Pearl Bailey, Miriam Hopkins, Ida Lupino, Jeanette MacDonald, Rita Hayworth, Gene Tierney, Cyd Charisse, Alfred Lunt, Richard Bennett, Gary Cooper, Fredric March, Walter Huston, William Holden, Tyrone Power, Henry Fonda, Brian Aherne, Mickey Rooney, Maurice Chevalier and Fred Astaire, not to mention one year's tryst on the Thames (which stood-in for Tiber) with Elizabeth Taylor in something called* Cleopatra. *Henry Fonda and Clifford Odets were extras in one play he directed; Katharine Hepburn made her first professional appearance in another. Bette Davis and Charlton Heston played their first important young leads in two others, and Myrna Loy changed type in still, still another. Mamoulian brought Elissa Landi to America and Claude Rains, Sylvia Sidney, William Holden, and Rita Hayworth to stardom. And so on, and so forth. Consequently, with Mamoulian, it is no longer a question of finding his way, but of retracing his steps and reviewing his grand strategies.*

It all began in Tiflis on 8 October 1899. Mamoulian was virtually born into the theatre on his mother's side. She was President of the Armenian Theatre in Tiflis. As a child, Mamoulian went to school at the Lycée Montaigne in Paris, where his family lived for several years. At that time he had two heroes: Napoleon and Buffalo Bill. Later he was graduated from high school in Tiflis and proceeded to the University of Moscow to study criminal law. Before long, he joined the Second Studio Theatre of the Moscow Art Theatre which held its sessions in the evenings under the direction of Eugene Vachtangov. After an interlude of functioning as drama critic on a newspaper in Tiflis, Mamoulian went to London. It was there that he began his professional career by directing The Beating on the Door, *a play by Austin Page, which opened at the St James's Theatre in November 1922 with an all-star cast.* – A.S.

MAMOULIAN: To direct a professional production in London at that early age was unprecedented. The management put into my contract a clause saying that whenever I was asked, in public or in print, as to how old I was, my answer should be: 'Around thirty.' A London paper carrying the first release of my engagement had a photograph of me with the caption: 'Mamoulian thirty but has tasted life.' How did this happen? I don't know; even now I find it hard to believe. It was a concatenation of unexpected circumstances, accidents, luck, destiny – whatever you choose to call it. It was not a time for encouraging youth, believe me.

In the direction of *The Beating on the Door*, I was totally under the influence of the Stanislavski method of the Moscow Art Theatre. You know, utter realism – chopping wood, real wood, naturalistic action, and all that. This was the first and last production that I directed in this manner. I discovered I had no affinity for naturalism on the stage. In my subsequent work, my aim always was rhythm and poetic stylization.

Anyway, I made one crucial choice at that time. Jacques Hébertot of the Théâtre des Champs-Elysées had offered me a post at his theatre as part of the trinity, which included Louis Jouvet and Theodor Komissarjevsky. At almost the same time, George Eastman (of Kodak) asked me to come to Rochester, New York, to help organize and direct the American Opera Company. I have never regretted the decision I made in chosing the land of Buffalo Bill. To me, the appeal of the 'New World' was irresistible.

While at Rochester, I directed in English such operas as *Carmen*, *Boris Godunov*, *Faust*, *Tannhäuser*, *Rigoletto*, *Pelléas and Mélisande* and others, as well as Viennese operettas and Gilbert and Sullivan. Then came Maurice Maeterlinck's *Sister Beatrice* in English, the first production in which I tried to integrate dialogue, music, and dance. I felt strongly that theatre at its fullest should utilize all forms of expression that come within its scope by harmoniously combining in one production dialogue, dramatic action, dance, song, and music.

From Rochester I went to New York, where I directed several 'straight' plays at the Theatre Guild School of Acting (*Seven Keys to Baldpate, He Who Gets Slapped, Enter Madame*, etc.). I 'arrived' you might say, on 10 October 1927, with *Porgy*, a play by DuBose and Dorothy Heyward. This was my first production for the Theatre Guild in New York. The New York drama critics of that time – Percy Hammond, Alexander Woollcott, Brooks Atkinson, Heywood Broun and others – gave it rave reviews. It ran for two and a half years in the United States, then was sent to London. Max Reinhardt referred to it in a published letter to Alexander Woolcott, as one of his greatest experiences in the theatre and a perfect example of utter stylization combined with psychological realism. Maurice Ravel, the composer called it 'the best opera' he had ever seen. Among the unusual high-spots in the production were: the four-minute-long scene of Catfish Row awakening in the morning, which consisted of gradual rhythmic progression of household noises (it became known as the 'symphony of noises'), and the lighting of the Negro wake scene resulting in a kind of ballet of huge shadows on the wall. The latter has been widely copied ever since. Reinhardt himself used it in Berlin in the production of *Burlesque*. In direction and staging, I used my favourite principle of integrating all theatrical elements into one stylized rhythmic pattern. I had developed this method during 1924, 1925, 1926 in Rochester, and later applied it to such Broadway productions as *Porgy and Bess*, 1935; *Oklahoma!*, 1943; *Carousel*, 1945; *St Louis Woman*, 1946; *Lost in the Stars*, 1949; and such movies as *Love Me Tonight*, 1932; *The Gay Desperado*, 1936; *Summer Holiday* (musical version of Eugene O'Neill's *Ah, Wilderness!*), 1948; *Silk Stockings*, 1957.

SARRIS: *How did you get into the movies?*

Jesse Lasky and Walter Wanger of Paramount engaged me for *Applause*. Actually, if I had had to go to Hollywood, it might have taken me years to leave Broadway, but Paramount was still making movies in its Astoria studio in 1929, so I broke into the movies without leaving New York, something you couldn't do later on. Anyway, I was one of those stage specialists they were hiring in those days to help the silent directors make sound movies. From the beginning of my career, I made it a policy never to sign a long-term contract with options. I hung around the set when Herbert Brenon made *Cinderella* and Jean Limur made a film with Jeanne Eagels. George Folsey, my cameraman on *Applause*, the sound engineer, even the head of the wardrobe department, all kept telling me what couldn't be done. It's curious really. Here I had been recruited as a stage expert on dialogue, and all I could think of was the marvellous things one could do with the camera and the exciting new potentials of sound recording. The camera fascinated me. Some theorists talk about the camera as a means of rendering reality. This is true; but the camera's greater and more glorious power is in its capacity of conveying truth through stylization and poetic rhythm.

Had you been influenced by any particular movies in the 20s?

That's a hard question to answer. As often as not, I was influenced negatively. That is to say that I would see something and think that's *not* the way to do it. I remember among the films that impressed me most favourably were Ernst Lubitsch's *The Marriage Circle* and F. W. Murnau's *The Last Laugh*.

You certainly didn't have any precedents to follow when you made Applause*?*

Indeed not. Everyone was against change, against rocking the boat, or rather, moving the camera or jiggling the sound. You have no idea how cumbersome sound and camera equipment was in the beginning. It was like walking around with a bungalow on your back. The camera

Helen Morgan in *Applause*

had to be enclosed in a booth so that the whirring of the motor didn’ get on the sound-track, and the sound technicians kept telling you tha ‘mixing’ was impossible. For a certain scene in *Applause*, I insisted o using two separate channels for recording two sounds: one, sof whispering; the other, loud singing; which later would be mixed, s that the audience could hear both simultaneously. It seems funn today when we use a multitude of channels that this was a revolutionar breakthrough. I had to fight for every innovation, for every camer movement. In those days, a scene was shot with three cameras, tw for close-ups, one for long-shot. And then into the cutting room t intercut the three. I insisted on a fluid camera which would pan freely as well as move in and out of a scene. George Folsey kept telling m that it couldn’t be done, but we did it, and he was very proud of it. also had trouble with keeping Helen Morgan in character as a blows burlesque queen. They kept wanting to pretty up everything – glamour you know.

Did you have any trouble with City Streets*?*

Not as much, but some. For instance, I was convinced that sound o

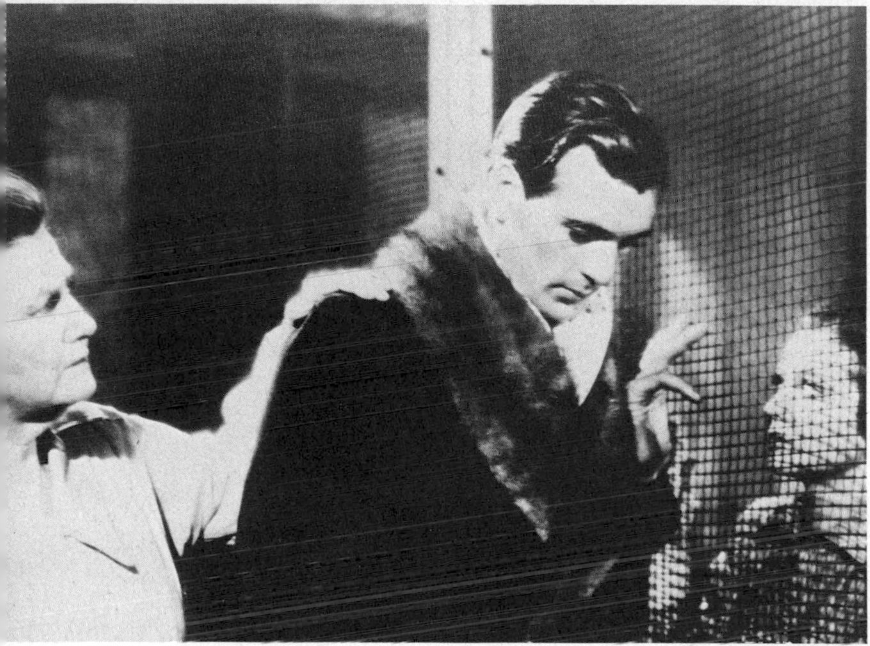

Gary Cooper in *City Streets*

the screen should not be constantly shackled by naturalism. The magic of sound recording enabled one to achieve effects that would be impossible and unnatural on the stage or in real life, yet meaningful and eloquent on the screen. I conceived the idea of running an audible sound-track over a silent close-up of Sylvia Sidney which would express her thoughts and memories. No one thought audiences would be able to accept this kind of audible inner monologues and reminiscences combined with a silent face. The audiences understood and accepted it quite easily. Here again, the film-makers were underestimating the public. Subsequently, of course, it became an important and frequently used device in film-making.

How did you achieve that fantastic final close-up of Garbo in Queen Christina*?*

That's a quaint story. I had quite an argument with L. B. Mayer on the ending of the film. He wanted a happy ending. This, to me, was unthinkable. Mr Mayer and his associates felt that the tragic ending would be depressing to the audience. I told him that I was as much against depressing audiences as he was but that tragedy in the theatre

Tea-break on the set of *Dr Jekyll and Mr Hyde*: Fredric March, Mamoulian, Miriam Hopkins

does not produce depression. I insisted on shooting the ending as I had conceived it. Then I would show it to Mr Mayer, and his other producers, and see if they still felt the ending was depressing. As you remember, the whole last sequence in *Queen Christina* is practically silent. It consists of a rhythmic progression of graphic images (ship sails, faces, pantomimic action) ending with Garbo's close-up. I was sure that the dramatic effect of this silent sequence would produce a feeling of exaltation, the classical catharsis. When Mr Mayer and all the big brass were shown the film in the projection room, nary a one of them mentioned depression; in fact, they were all exhilarated. My trump in this was the final close-up of Garbo's face, which began with a long view and ended with an enormous close-up that ran for eighty-five feet. I gambled much on this last shot. Again, the technicians said it couldn't be done. The dilemma was that the long-shot at the start required a wide-angle lens, while the close-up at the end called for a four- or six-inch lens. It was obvious that I had to use a wide-angle lens which would have to come within a few inches of Garbo's face to achieve the final close-up. For this, I needed a device which would progressively modify the degrees of diffusion as the camera rolled in.

There was the rub – no such device existed at that time. (Today, of course, it is child's play.) We were stuck. Suddenly an early childhood memory popped into my mind when my parents gave me a magic lantern for Christmas. I thought of that long glass slide on which there were four separate pictures that could be projected on a white sheet or a wall by gradually moving the glass slide in front of the lens. That was it – all we needed was a similar piece of glass on which, instead of pictures, there would be graduated diffusions. The laboratory went to work and the new gadget was ready by five o'clock. Garbo always stopped shooting at five; this time, however, she stayed until seven. We made two takes: one was no good; the other was perfect. The rest, as we say, is history.

What did you tell her to think of when she was staring into the camera?

Ah, that is precisely the question she asked me: 'What do I express in this last shot?' My answer was: 'Nothing; absolutely nothing. You must make your mind and your heart a complete blank. Make your face into a mask; do not even blink your eyes while the camera is on you.' You see, with a tragic ending like this, no matter what feelings are portrayed by the actress, and these could range from hysterical sobs to a smile, some of the audience would disagree, find them wrong. This was one of those marvellous spots where a film could turn every spectator into a creator. If the face is blank, just like John Locke's *tabula rasa*, then every member of the audience inevitably will write in his own emotions. Thus, the 'expression' would be true for every spectator because it is created by him. Incidentally, some of the scenes in *Queen Christina* were shot to a metronome – to achieve a rhythmic quality akin to a dance. You may recall the scene of Miss Garbo saying goodbye to her room at the inn – that was a graphic poem.

What do you think of current trends in movies and the theatre?

Theatre of the Absurd, the *Nouvelle Vague*, Improvisation, *Avant-garde*, etc.?

Yes.

Actually, there is little new about all this. *Avant-garde* has existed in every generation. It starts out with much sound and fury, but before you know it, its iconoclastic passions settle into a conformism of their own. One good thing has been achieved: the breaking down of rigid, conventional forms of movie-making.

I think today films, not unlike other arts, suffer from psychic depression. Ours is a peculiar age – while scientists are lifting man into space, most artists keep shoving him into the gutter. Too many film-makers seem obsessed with human foibles, illnesses, and frustrations. Also, the crowning absurdity: after millions of years of evolution we are 'discovering' sex, violence, cruelty. The claim is that this is life, this is truth. Not so; half-truths at best. Noble impulses and 'immortal longings' are also a part of human nature. Art must be concerned with the whole truth, not just its sickly fragments. Also, too frequently people tend to confuse novelty with originality, fad with achievement, slogans with principles.

The future? I am optimistic about it. The screen is the most powerful, exciting, and contemporary medium. One of these days we will learn to do it full justice.

Rouben Mamoulian: films as director

1929: *Applause*
1931: *City Streets*
1932: *Dr Jekyll and Mr Hyde, Love me Tonight*
1933: *Song of Songs, Queen Christina*
1934: *We live Again*
1935: *Becky Sharp*
1936: *The Gay Desperado*
1937: *High, Wide and Handsome*
1939: *Golden Boy*
1940: *The Mark of Zorro*
1941: *Blood and Sand*
1942: *Rings on Her Fingers*
1947: *Summer Holiday*
1957: *Silk Stockings*

Otto Preminger talking to Ian Cameron, Mark Shivas and Paul Mayersberg, 1965

The next film Otto Preminger directs will be his thirtieth in an American career that goes back thirty years. There are certain ifs, ands and buts in these calculations, however. Preminger refuses to accept any responsibility whatsoever for the films he made before Laura *in 1944, which was twenty-one years ago. These earlier films are* Under Your Spell *(1936),* Danger – Love at Work *(1937),* Margin for Error *(1943), and* In the Meantime, Darling *(1944). Preminger is not unique in disdaining the fruits of his early experience. Fred Zinnemann has never been eager to reminisce about* Kid Glove Killer, Eyes in the Night, Little Mr Jim *and* My Brother Talks to Horses. *George Stevens undoubtedly prefers to jump straight to* Alice Adams *without pausing for* Cohens and Kellys in Trouble, Bachelor Bait *and* Kentucky Kernels. *Vincente Minnelli's mystique does not encompass* I Dood It *any more than Robert Aldrich's boasts of* The Big Leaguer, *and Josef von Sternberg would probably prefer to forget his close-up of Grace Moore's tonsils in* The King Steps Out.

It is only within the past decade that American directors have been taken seriously en masse *and* in toto. *Consequently, more than a few feel that they have been caught with slips showing in their careers. It was* so much easier in those old days, when a director was no better than his last picture, and no worse. Today, all his films are weighed on the critical scales, and so his place in film history may be jeopardized by a piece of hoke he shot to pay off the mortgage on his Hollywood hacienda.

Not that Preminger's pre-Laura films are particularly shameful, and it can be argued that nothing he has done since Laura has clicked quite so completely as Laura on every level of evaluation. Nor can it be argued that the director has either soared or sunk since he left Fox in the early 50s to become his own producer. Ironically, it was only when Preminger began blowing his own horn from The Moon Is Blue onwards that his earlier films came into focus. His enemies have never forgiven him for being a director with the personality of a producer. His more discerning detractors subconsciously resent him for not ruining himself with the excesses of a creative folly. Culture heroes like Von Sternberg and Von Stroheim and Ophuls and Welles have acquired, rightly or wrongly, a legendary reputation for profligacy. Preminger's legend is that of the cosmic cost-accountant, a ruthless creature who will mangle the muse for the sake of a shooting schedule.

The story is told in the trade of the day Preminger shot the Saint-Newman hilltop scene in Exodus. During the last take, the shadow of the boom fell across the couple. It was too late for a re-take, because the sun was going. Preminger decided to let the shadow stand rather than to return to the location the next day, for a retake, disrupting his shooting schedule. Some finicky aesthetes might write this off as sloppy craftsmanship, but for Preminger it is a question of survival. The fact that he can bring a spectacle in for three million or under, while his colleagues come in for seven or eleven, explains why Preminger is still making his own pictures and why Zinnemann has gone back to work for a studio.

The fact is that Preminger has not had a real critical and commercial smash since Anatomy of a Murder some years ago. His frugality, and his frugality alone, has kept him from drowning in a sea of red ink. Almost alone of the new tribe of producer-directors, Preminger has accepted the responsibility of freedom, as well as the lesson of a shrinking market.

But what is the artistic point of all these crass production stories? Or as Dwight Macdonald might put it, what's art to Preminger or Preminger to art? Preminger's champions on Movie and Cahiers du Cinéma would retort that Preminger's art is of the highest order. I find myself in a dangerous middle position that I would like to explain in some detail. To do so, I must begin with a very personal definition of mise en scène.

For me, mise en scène is not merely the gap between what we see and feel on the screen and what we can express in words, but it is also the gap *between the intention of the director and his effect upon the spectator. Serious film criticism of Hollywood movies is always impaled upon the point that Hollywood directors are not profoundly articulate about their alleged art. How can one possibly compare John Ford to Michelangelo Antonioni, for example? Antonioni talks like an intellectual, albeit a middle-brow intellectual, while Ford talks like an old prospector cut off from civilization. American critics travel abroad bemoaning the fact that American directors are unable to conduct festival seminars on the Pressing Problems of Our Time. Certainly any three Polish directors you might pick up in the street would undoubtedly out-pontificate and out-paradox the legions of Hollywood directors from time immemorial.*

In this respect, Preminger is not a 'good' interview. He will freely concede that more is read into his films by some critics than he consciously put there. He neither abuses his detractors nor embraces his defenders. He seems to enjoy the effect he creates with his outrageous personality, a personality that serves also as a mask. To read all sorts of poignant profundities in Preminger's inscrutable urbanity would seem to be the last word in idiocy, and yet there are moments in his films when the evidence on the screen is inconsistent with one's deepest instincts about the director as a man. It is during these moments that one feels the magical powers of mise en scène *to get more out of a picture than is put in by a director.*

However, I would not go as far in this regard as Michel Mourlet of the MacMahon Theatre, where Preminger's portrait once occupied a prominent position in the lobby with Fritz Lang, Joseph Losey and Raoul Walsh. (I don't know what has happened to the theatre, or to the lobby display, since the MacMahonists split into rival Preminger and Losey factions.) It is Mourlet's contention that Preminger must be judged entirely by the effects that the director creates on the screen rather than by any cultural precedents off the screen. To be more exact, Preminger's Saint Joan *should be judged entirely by the light patterns on the screen making up the images of Preminger's* mise en scène *rather than by Preminger's fidelity to some interplanetary literary source in the Shavian galaxy. According to Mourlet, the screen creates its own laws independent of the other arts, and the literary and historical Joan of Arc is less important than the way Preminger renders his Jean of Iowa.*

The trouble with Mourlet's position, tempting as it seems, is that the nature of movies as we have known them, particularly from Hollywood, involves an objective core on which the subjective styles of directors can operate. It is Preminger's manner, rather than his matter, which should concern us most deeply. Otherwise, his extraordinary electicism in subject matter would make him a poor choice indeed for a career article.

What is one to say of a taste in scripts oscillating between Oscar Wilde and Kathleen Winsor, George Bernard Shaw and F. Hugh Herbert, Nelson Algren and Allen Drury, Françoise Sagan and Leon Uris? Some of his defenders argue that he must be commended for tackling the big subjects, but if Preminger is to get a medal for bravely tackling the Big Subject, Stanley Kramer should get a chest-full.

No. It is not a consistent theme we must look for in appraising Preminger's career, but a consistent attitude. One critic has called it fairness, another the ambiguity of objectivity. I would prefer to stress the perversely objective camera viewpoint that keeps his characters in the same frame. Why does Preminger present his spectacle in this way? As he himself explains, he came from the theatre where he was accustomed to looking at drama as a spatial whole. Consequently, his deepest instincts are always opposed to montage. Without an inbred instinct for cutting, he is not able to execute the movie gags for which Hollywood has developed an elaborate original cinematographic language. It follows almost logically that Preminger's subjects, more often than not, have a solemn, sombre quality. His melodramas at Fox, particularly Laura, Fallen Angel, Whirlpool, Where the Sidewalk Ends, *and his RKO loan-out,* Angel Face, *are all moodily fluid studies in perverse psychology rather than crackling suspense movies. The characters click even as the action falters. The reviewer in search of crackling melodrama would mark Preminger down as a failure in most of these films, possibly all except* Laura. *Even his comedies are too fluid to encompass the inevitable reaction shots.* The Moon Is Blue *comes out being a little sad, and* Bonjour Tristesse, *far from being a merry Gallic romp, is transformed by Preminger's colour/black-and-white duality into a tragedy of time and illusion.*

It might be said that where Richard Brooks displays a tendency to transform art into trash, Preminger displays a tendency to transform trash into art. His plots lately have been big, violent and vulgar. Exodus, Advise and Consent, The Cardinal *and* In Harm's Way *have enough holes in their scenarios for a ton of Swiss cheese. Preminger does not entirely transcend his material on any occasion. For one thing, his players are too uneven. John Wayne and Patricia Neal are truly admirable in* In Harm's Way, *but Paula Prentiss, Tom Tryon and Patrick O'Neal are truly deplorable. For every John Huston in* The Cardinal *there is unfortunately a Lee J. Cobb in* Exodus. *Individual scenes can be magnificent – the prison raid in* Exodus, *the shipboard sequences with the President in* Advise and Consent, *the Viennese ballroom scene in* The Cardinal, *and the opening dance scene in* In Harm's Way *invoking in one slowly moving shot the entire* Zeitgeist *of the 40s. Too often, how-*

ever, Preminger seems to destroy what he so lovingly creates. This is part of his ambiguity as an artist, a key perhaps to a cynicism far deeper and infinitely more destructive than Billy Wilder's.

I am not suggesting that Preminger has ever thrown a game or even consciously shaved the points. Every Preminger film, even his most ill-fated, bears the signs of an overall conception and the stigmata of a personal attitude. If a Centennial Summer or a Porgy and Bess fails to come off, it is not because Preminger lacked a discernible approach towards these musicals, but rather because the various elements in the musicals failed to coalesce in terms of Preminger's conception. By contrast, Carmen Jones succeeds on its own questionable terms as the Preminger musical par excellence – drab, austere, unpleasant and completely depoeticized.

In his career Preminger has moved into direct competition or comparison with other directors. A Royal Scandal and The Fan pointed up Preminger's relationship to Lubitsch, as did obviously That Lady in Ermine, which Preminger finished after Lubitsch's death. Lubitsch is generally given the edge in these sectors, and for good reason. However, it is not entirely fair to Preminger to place him out of his time. As Lubitsch was the unobtrusive cutting of the 20s and 30s, Preminger is the camera movement and long takes of the 50s and 60s. If Lubitsch summed up this time, Preminger was ahead of it in his Fox period. The Lubitsch virtues have disappeared from the cinema, and we are the poorer for it, but Preminger anticipated the conditions that would cause their disappearance. The grace and precision of Lubitsch's sensibility seem out of place in a world consecrated to the most grotesque explosions of the ego. Preminger's impassive gaze – accepting the good with the bad, the beautiful with the ugly, the sublime with the mediocre – is both more appropriate and more merciful.

Preminger himself refuses to allow any comparison between The Thirteenth Letter and the Clouzot original, Le Corbeau (The Raven), but it might be noted parenthetically that Preminger's version is less vicious than the original, and not merely because of the laundered Hollywood script. Preminger has no patience with the virus of suspicion, and he tends to give the show away rather than to degrade his characters with useless doubts.

With In Harm's Way, Preminger invades the realm of John Ford, with curious results. A combination of They Were Expendable and Wings of Eagles, the Preminger film departs from the Ford ethos of the military by dramatizing the conflict over strategy between the aggressive Wayne and the defensive Dana Andrews, that ageing Preminger alumnus of Laura, Fallen Angel, Daisy Kenyon, Where the Sidewalk

Ends. *On the surface, the Wayne side has all the best of it. Andrews and his entourage are virtually caricatured while Wayne is being idealized. Wayne's spoiled rotten Harvard son, Brandon De Wilde, is used as the swing character to indicate the complete collapse of the Andrews arguments. Preminger seems to have succumbed at last to bias, if only the bias in favour of action in the abstract. However, a second look indicates that Wayne wins every argument and loses every battle, and that catastrophe dogs him every step of the way. Once more Preminger has stepped aside from a commitment, and the result is less satisfying intellectually than either Ford's whole-hearted commitment to the institution or Kubrick's giddily anarchistic disrespect for it in* Dr Strangelove.

Where does this all leave us? It leaves us with a director who has made at least three impressive masterpieces of ambiguity and objectivity – Laura, Bonjour Tristesse *and* Advise and Consent, *a director who sees all problems and issues as a single-take two-shot, the stylistic expression of the eternal conflict not between right and wrong but between the right-wrong on one side and the right-wrong on the other, a representation of the right-wrong in all of us as our share of the human condition. In the middle of the conflict stands Otto Preminger, right-wrong, good-bad and probably sincere-cynical. But don't take my word for it. See the movies and make up your own mind. Whatever your verdict, Preminger will thank you for your patronage and will keep his own counsels.* – A.S.

CAMERON: *Why did you choose to make* In Harm's Way*?*

PREMINGER: Why do I ever want to make a film? This book was submitted to me in manuscript. I liked the characters and I liked the story. This is my only reason for making films. It is my profession to make films.

However, there is another reason. Probably the story appealed to me because I felt that so many movies made recently have a terribly pessimistic outlook on our future. It seems that the only way out for us is to give in to almost any kind of demand, or blackmail, or whatever you want to call it – and when I say 'us' it goes for both sides, for the West as well as for the Iron Curtain, because both have the Bomb now And all these films or books seem to feel that any attack would finish the other side, and the world. I don't believe that. I believe that any attack that is executed by weapons invented by people, by human minds, will always find a defence that people can invent. Perhaps this story of an attack – we are attacked, we are unprepared in every way and manage by sheer guts, character and resourcefulness, to start to work out of it – should remind us and perhaps other people that ther is never any reason to give up or to give in to anything that is not right or dignified. I am as much against the war as anyone, and I hope I showed it even in this picture by showing that, of all these courageous people, just two or three are left in the end. I didn't try to make war romantic or particularly attractive, but, on the other hand, I wanted to say, perhaps unlike other people, that war does not necessarily bring the worst out in people always. It often does, but also, for the mere reason that people find themselves in the same predicament, it makes them stick together, work for each other, work together.

I don't like to mention other films, but to mention one which I think is a very wonderful film – *Dr Strangelove* – I do feel that somehow it shows the situation only from one side. Perhaps the director, whom I like very much and admire, didn't want to show it. It cannot be true (and the film seems to imply this), that every military man in the United States is a warmonger or an idiot, or both, or crazy. Nor is it true that the President of the United States is so completely without sense. I don't mind these characters in satire – I think it is very good if there were some *balance* to it. Perhaps it could be told in another film. Let's say I don't tell my story *against* a film like *Strangelove*, I tell it to complement the film. You see, I feel that all films together, or the whole output of literature together, give a mosaic of the thinking and feeling of people. So it doesn't matter whether one film goes all the way one side and another film goes all the way the other side. It might be that people who see my film will wonder why I didn't show a character like the General in *Dr Strangelove* – although I tried to show that the Navy has not only angels.

When you get a large book like In Harm's Way, *you have to leave out a fair amount of the detail of it.*

Let me say something which I have always wanted to say but never could say quite clearly. Whether I take an original idea and pay for it, or I buy the rights to a book, and an author sells it outright, I consider this raw material and I feel completely free to use it according to my own thinking – to filter it through my own brain, through my talent or whatever I have, in other words, to re-create whatever part of this material I want to. This thing about being faithful or not faithful to a novel should only apply if the author would say: 'Look, I don't want to sell you the film rights, I want to be your *partner*. I will sell you the film rights with the condition that I have the final say, because I want to preserve the ideas.' I have often been attacked: the author of *Exodus* for instance felt that I didn't do right by his book, and the author of *Anatomy of a Murder* felt that I did better than the book –

Preminger and Richard Widmark on the set of *St Joan*

he admired the film very much. The author of *In Harm's Way* is particularly complimentary about my handling of the son's character, one which didn't really exist in his book. He was a completely innocuous boy, who just met the father and they immediately became friends; he had no feelings about the fact that his father had left his mother eighteen years ago, and we changed that in the script. Now, all I want to say is that I consider it material and I use what I want. In the book *In Harm's Way*, there is a lot about command decision and the great responsibility. This is interesting, but very difficult to dramatize and hardly a point that interested me here, because I'm not interested in the military mind really. I did not make a war picture – I don't know anything about the war, and I hope I will never see another war. It was more interesting to see a group of people, characters whom I like, trapped in war, in a difficult situation, and to see how they work out of it.

Why did you use Wendell Mayes?

I think he's a very good writer. We have worked together before and I felt that he could write this very well. You must realize also that I work very closely with writers. Particularly on this picture, we sat together and worked almost every line over. On the other hand, the writer has the advantage that, once I approve a screenplay, I do not change it any more on the set like other directors, or hire other writers to improve it or, as the case may be, to spoil it.

How far did the original book In Harm's Way *delve into the political aspect, which is slightly evident in the film through the Dana Andrews character?*

The Dana Andrews character is unimportant – it is just a question of one group of people wanting to fight, and the other group of people wanting to give up. We all probably forget this (and you are probably even too young to remember), but you know, after Pearl Harbor, there was in America a tremendous group of people of any political affiliation that thought the best thing would be to make peace with Japan and not to enter the war, that we were not prepared and that we would lose. And it seems very crazy today, but at that time people in San Francisco started to move out to the East, because they felt the Japanese might land at San Francisco. I don't think that the Dana Andrews character *is* to do with anything political. But it's typical. It shows the people making use of their power, and you must admit that the fact that I could get co-operation from the Defence Department, in spite of this character, in spite of Dana Andrews, and in spite

In Harm's Way

of the character of Kirk Douglas, proves a certain liberal attitude. I got all the ships I needed and all the help I needed, otherwise I couldn't have made this picture. We were shooting five days on the high seas between Seattle and Hawaii on a real naval cruiser with an Admiral there – it was his flagship – and he was lying there on his stomach most of the time taking photographs of us because it was his hobby.

How was it that your model shots were so much better than anyone else's model shots?

I will tell you a secret. I had originally hired a famous specialist for these models. You know, they usually make them with ships about two to three feet long, in tanks. When I saw the beginning of his work, which was also quite expensive, I threw the whole thing away because it didn't seem to be right. And I then proceeded to build ships, I did it myself after the picture was finished. I decided to direct it myself without any specialists, and we built ships that were between thirty-five and fifty-five feet long – they were really big ships – so that when we photographed them, the detail was very much like on the big ships. And as a matter of fact, the Navy asked us, and we gave them these

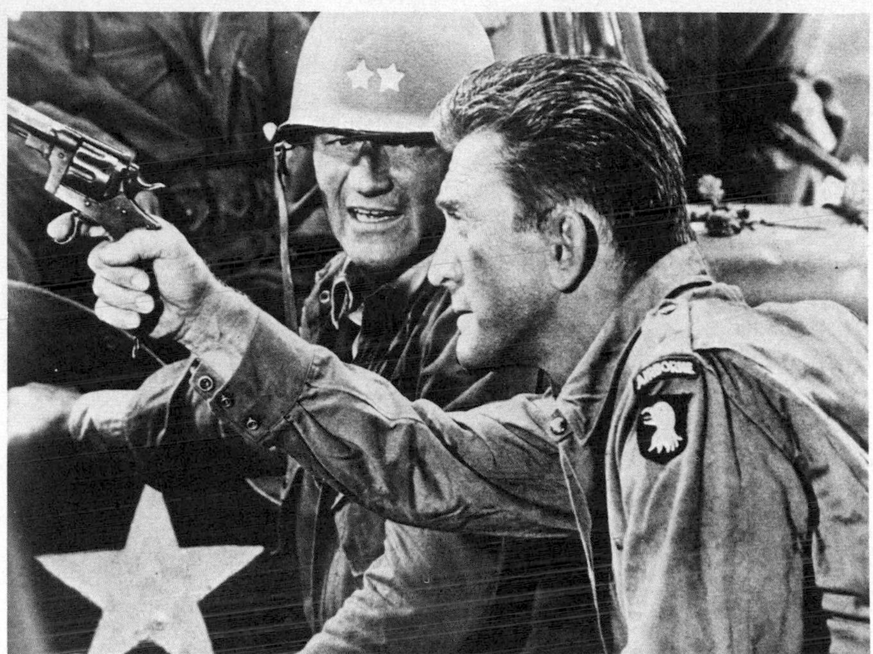

In Harm's Way: John Wayne, Kirk Douglas

ships after the picture was finished for their various exhibitions. And we didn't shoot any of these miniatures in a tank. We shot the night miniatures on a lake in Mexico, because we needed the straits with mountains in the background. We shot the day battles on the Gulf of Mexico. I needed the real horizon, you know, and I think that makes a lot of difference.

Is it because of the models that you didn't shoot the picture in colour?

No, I could just as well have shot it in colour. The reason I didn't is because I always feel that a picture like this, a war picture, in colour, has a very unreal feeling. First of all, you cannot possibly avoid the actors using make-up, particularly if they are close to middle age. A soldier in make-up always seems to me somewhat ridiculous. I know that people overlook it, that it is a convention that they accept, but a picture like this has much more impact and you can create more of the feeling, the illusion of reality than when you shoot it in colour. It's the only reason I didn't use any newsreel shots. For Pearl Harbor I got permission and put dynamite all around, and we shot this with real ships and real explosions. We didn't use any of the old stuff, because that was shown in so many pictures that I felt to show the same news clips again (because they're all the same) would be ridiculous.

In the first shot of In Harm's Way, *you start with the notice, then go past the line of caps and along the side of the swimming pool to Barbara Bouchet dancing: I suppose it's possible, in theory, to do this in a number of cut shots, although you get a much smoother idea of getting into the story by doing it in one shot. Is that why you do it in one shot?*

If it were possible, I would do the whole of the film in one shot, because I believe that every cut, no matter how carefully it is done, is disturbing. You may want to emphasize something through the cut (the cut is also a way to point up something), otherwise every cut is only done because you cannot tell something in one shot. You feel a cut subconsciously. There the idea was to show that this was what was going on just before Pearl Harbor: by putting in the sound of some vessels in the background, and the parking space, the announcement of the dance, the Navy hats on the long table, and the dance. Then when she behaves like she does, there are cuts and the story starts. This is already a character in the story. In order not to disturb this, I put the titles at the end, because I felt I wanted to get into the story right away and not to have all the usual clutter. I also wanted to make a point, which I don't know if people get, because they usually get up before the titles are finished: the titles go up to the atom bomb and show the future horror of possible war.

Does it make any difference to you making a film for Paramount as opposed to, say, Columbia or United Artists?

No. They only distribute the film; they have no influence on the making of my films. My contracts give me complete autonomy in the making, the casting and the writing. They can turn down a certain property if they don't want to make it, but once we've agreed on that, they have no more say.

It's good for you to ring the changes among distributors?

Sometimes . . . they are all very nice people!

Bunny Lake *is going to be a completely different kind of film?*

Bunny Lake is a suspense story. It's the first suspense story I've made in a long, long time, about twenty years. It's the story of the disappearance of a child.

Why are you making it here?

First of all, it seems to me that the farther away from home the mother who loses the child is, the more real the story seems. Every mystery story, you see, naturally has some holes, and it seems more

Bunny Lake is Missing: Carol Lynley

believable that certain facts cannot be checked within the ten hours in which the story takes place. Also the horror of what happens to her seems to be stronger if she's away from home. Even in the original book she is away from home; it takes place in New York. But I felt that this change would be an advantage. I had several scripts on this property. I have had this book for a long time and I never could get the right script out of it. I wanted her to be so lost. Originally, I wanted to do it in Paris, and she didn't speak French. But this problem seemed almost insurmountable because then the police would have to ask everything through an interpreter. That would be too difficult. So I took it here to London. I can probably also get more interesting actors to surround these two young people here than in America. We have a great shortage of really good character actors.

You said you went through several scripts. What were you after that you couldn't get?

The original book has a very weak solution. The solution is OK, but the character who commits the crime is very weak and uninteresting. We did the first script very much like the book. I did this with

Ira Levin, a playwright who wrote the play that I did with Henry Fonda, *Critic's Choice*. Then I did another script with Dalton Trumbo. We had analysed it and found that we needed another heavy but he became very theatrical and wrong. When you talk, it is often very different from what happens when you actually write and dramatize it. I gave up this script. Eventually when I wanted to do it here, I sent the book to Penelope Mortimer because she is a novelist, and I told her what the trouble was: she came to New York for conferences and came up with a wonderful character, I think, of a heavy, which gave the whole picture a new dimension. That made me pick it up again. Then she and her husband wrote the present screenplay except for some polishing on American dialogue which I had somebody else do. As a matter of fact, I have had the rights to this story so long that somebody said that Bunny Lake is not missing, Bunny Lake is legally dead!

What will you make after that?

A book that I bought about nine months ago; it was published in America about six or seven weeks ago. It's called *Hurry Sundown*, by B.K. Gilden. They're really two people, married, and they worked for fourteen years on this book. And as a matter of fact they were so poor on the way that the husband had to work in a factory in order to support the family. The book has become a very big best seller in the United States. It has a very broad canvas. It takes place in 1946 in Georgia, and shows all the problems of the Negroes and the white people and their relationships. Some critics call it a modern *Gone with the Wind*. And again, while it has no message, no immediate, present political message, it will, I think, show that all the things that happen now – Civil Rights and riots – this whole revolution had to come. It was the only way to solve it.

In The Cardinal *there was a tremendous compression of history into one story. How far was it this aspect rather than the central character that excited you?*

These questions become too specific, because making a film is a complete complex of things. Naturally the background was very interesting. It is the background of history but also the background of an institution like the Church and what was going on in it. I have found that the Catholic Church is really a fabulously interesting institution. It gives its various members much more autonomy than I thought before. I am not a Catholic. I don't know if it comes out in the picture – but I started to understand why the Catholic Church, in spite of always reasserting its moral purpose or at least returning to its principles, is able by compromise to survive almost any other institution and organization. You see now their willingness to get together with non-Catholics, even with non-believers, which shows that they somehow realize the needs of progressing times. They are not really as conservative or reactionary as most people believe. That interested me very much.

Surely these are last minute changes though?

No. It is clear that any organization would hang on to its principles as long as it could, just as the monarchy in England has survived all other monarchies, because it is the most liberal monarchy and gives people the right to change their government, under the Crown. The Catholic Church, too, always knows the right moment to compromise.

How much do you rehearse a scene on the floor?

That depends very much on what is necessary, on what kind of actor and what kind of scene. You see certain kinds of pictures – in *Advise and Consent*, for instance, or *Anatomy of a Murder*, there were scenes that I rehearsed several weeks before I started, but other pictures, like for instance *In Harm's Way*, cannot be rehearsed in advance because I cannot go out on the ship, you know, and it doesn't make sense to read these lines in a room. So I rehearse just before I do the scene and I rehearse as long as necessary. There is no limit. Time is expensive and naturally in the back of one's mind; one cannot completely eliminate it, but I've educated myself just to forget it. Otherwise the whole thing becomes hurried and silly. I could make every picture ten days shorter if I slough it. Some actors just need more time and more rehearsal and some don't. Some actors, who are basically picture personalities, cannot rehearse. They become what they call stale. Really it is because they don't quite know what they are doing. You've got to catch them when they are doing it best. Some actors need a lot of rehearsal and those are very good actors.

You use a lot of long takes for dialogue scenes. Do you, as it were, let the actors dictate the length of the shot?

No. The actors don't dictate anything. Sometimes you have an actor who can't remember more than two lines. There comes the moment where you have to compromise and give in, but usually it is not the case, because scenes are not that long. No scene can be longer than nine and a half minutes, because that's how long the film runs in the camera. Six minutes or five minutes most actors are capable of doing. Once in my career I had a difficulty like that with a seasoned actor, but otherwise I don't remember ever having difficulty.

Presumably with actors like Wayne and Douglas who are personalities you didn't have to rehearse much.

No, that isn't true. Wayne turned out – I have not worked with him before – to be the most co-operative actor, willing to rehearse, willing to do anything as long as anybody. I was surprised really, how disciplined a professional Wayne is, and he liked this particular part very much. I must say, I am very lucky this way, you know, the actors I work with are not difficult or I am more difficult than they are so that I don't notice!

Otto Preminger: films as director

1936: *Under Your Spell*
1937: *Danger – Love at Work*
1943: *Margin for Error*
1944: *In the Meantime Darling, Laura*
1945: *A Royal Scandal (Czarina), Fallen Angel*
1946: *Centennial Summer*
1947: *Forever Amber, Daisy Kenyon*
1948: *That Lady in Ermine* (begun and signed by Lubitsch)
1949: *The Fan*
1950: *Whirlpool, Where the Sidewalk Ends*
1951: *The Thirteenth Letter*
1952: *Angel Face*
1953: *The Moon is Blue*
1954: *River of No Return, Carmen Jones*
1955: *The Court-Martial of Billy Mitchell (One Man Mutiny), The Man with the Golden Arm*
1957: *Saint Joan*
1958: *Bonjour Tristesse*
1959: *Porgy and Bess, Anatomy of a Murder*
1960: *Exodus*
1962: *Advise and Consent*
1963: *The Cardinal*
1965: *In Harm's Way, Bunny Lake is Missing*
1966: *Hurry Sundown*
1968: *Skidoo*
1970: *Tell Me That You Love Me, Junie Moon*

Preston Sturges recalled by Andrew Sarris, 1962

Acknowledged as the foremost satirist of his time, Preston Sturges enjoyed his greatest vogue between 1940 and 1944 when his pungent wit and frenetic slapstick exploded on such topics as Tammany Hall politics, advertising, American fertility rites, hero and mother worship. Within the context of a Sturges film, a gangster could declare with ringing, heavily accented conviction: 'America is a land of great opportunity.' An underpaid clerk could rise to fame and fortune by coining the slogan: 'If you can't sleep, it isn't the coffee, it's the bunk!' A sign in a flophouse could remind its denizens: 'Have you written to mother?' Sturges repeatedly suggested that the lowliest boob could rise to the top with the right degree of luck, bluff, and fraud. The absurdity of the American success story was matched by the ferocity of the battle of the sexes. In The Lady Eve, *when Henry Fonda plaintively confesses: 'Snakes are my life,' Barbara Stanwyck snaps back: 'What a life!' The climax of* Palm Beach Story *finds Rudy Vallee serenading Claudette Colbert's upstairs window while the object of his affections is being seduced by the subject of hers, Joel McCrea.*

Sturgean comedy was influenced both by the silent antics of Charles Chaplin, Buster Keaton, and Harold Lloyd in the 20s, and by the

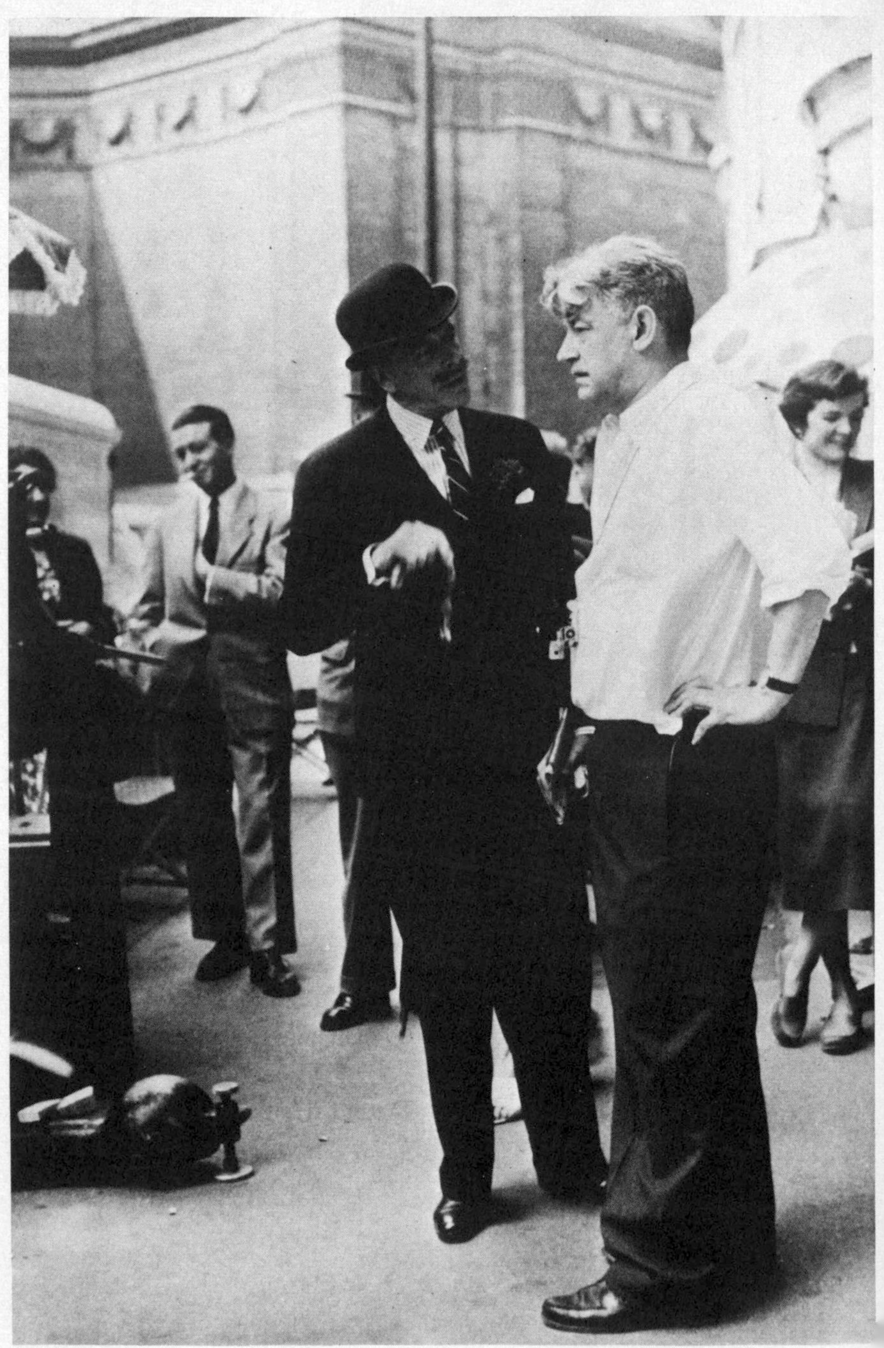

Jack Buchanan and Preston Sturges on the set of *Les Carnets du Major Thompson*

crackling verbal rhythms of Howard Hawks, Frank Capra, Leo McCarey and Gregory La Cava in the 30s. Sturges contributed to this distinguished tradition mainly through the unusual density of his scripts. His films were noted for the hilarious side effects of character and bit actors. It was not unusual for a gravel-voiced bus driver to use the word, 'paraphrase', nor for a hoodlum to invoke the ruinous symmetry of 'Samson and Delilah, Sodom and Gomorrah'. A stereotyped performer like Eric Blore was virtually rediscovered savouring the line: 'I positively swill in his ale.' Similarly, Edgar Kennedy was resurrected from two-reelers to play an inspired bartender reacting to a customer asking for his first drink ever: 'Sir, you rouse the artist in me.' The Sturges stock company was particularly noted for the contrasting personalities of William Demarest, the eternal roughneck, and Franklin Pangborn, the eternal snob.

Sturges was criticized at the time by James Agee, Manny Farber, and other reputable critics for an ambivalence in his work projected from a childhood conflict between a culturally demanding mother and an admired businessman foster father. This unusually Freudian analysis of the director's work sought to explain the incongruity of continental sophistication being challenged by American pragmatism. Sturges himself was seen as an uneasy mixture of savant and wise guy. On the one hand, his extreme literacy, rare among Hollywood screenwriters, enabled him to drop words like 'ribaldry' and 'vestal' into their proper contexts without a pretentious thud. On the other, he seemed unwilling to develop the implications of his serious ideas. His flair for props and gadgets suited the popularly recalled image of the young inventor of kissproof lipstick.

His reputation today is based mainly on the eight films he directed for Paramount. The Great McGinty, *a vigorous satire of big-city politics marked by lusty performances from Akim Tamiroff as the Boss and Brian Donlevy as the hobo elevated to governor, was the pilot film of the writer-director movement in Hollywood. Most directors had previously risen from the ranks of studio technicians and stage directors. After Sturges led the way, John Huston, Billy Wilder, Dudley Nichols, Clifford Odets, Nunnally Johnson, Robert Rossen, Samuel Fuller, Frank Tashlin, and Blake Edwards followed from the writer's cubicle to the director's chair.* Christmas in July *lingered over a Depression mood as Dick Powell and Ellen Drew played an engaged couple trying to make ends meet on a combined salary of forty dollars a week. The vagaries of luck and the cruelty of practical jokes developed the plot in what was to be later recognized as the distinctive and disturbing Sturges manner.* The Lady Eve, *a sophisticated comedy with Henry Fonda and Barbara*

Stanwyck, was hailed by The New York Times as the best film of 1941. Sturges circumvented the censors with a rowdy blackout technique that began where the more discreet 'Lubitsch touch' had left off. An adroit manipulation of mistaken identity aided Sturges in preserving the technical morality of the marriage contract. The duet in The Lady Eve was later enlarged into the quadrille of Palm Beach Story in which Joel McCrea, Claudette Colbert, Mary Astor, and Rudy Vallee were perpetually confused and obsessed by the permutations of what Sturges leeringly defined as 'Subject A'.

Sullivan's Travels, a Swiftian glimpse of Hollywood and its occasional flirtations with social consciousness, is generally considered the most profound expression of the director's personality. Dedicating the film to the world's clowns and mountebanks, Sturges forthrightly defended the muse of comedy against the presumably more serious demands of society. Like Shakespeare's Winter's Tale, the film pivots in one dance-like moment from comedy to tragedy when an old derelict is trapped in a metal jungle of switch rails and is unable to evade an oncoming train. The Miracle at Morgan's Creek and Hail the Conquering Hero represented the director's original vision of small-town America within which Eddie Bracken emerged as a Sturges folk hero. In Miracle, Bracken has 'greatness thrust upon him' when his frolicsome V-girl sweetheart, Betty Hutton, is thoughtful enough to transcend her disgrace with sextuplets. In Hero, Bracken survives the ordeal of a 4-F self-exposed as a false war hero, and again he is redeemed by the generous emotions of his girl friend, Ella Raines. Many critics were impressed by the intense performance of ex-prizefighter Freddie Steele, in the film an orphanage-bred marine hero with a severe mother complex.

After 1944, when he left Paramount to form a short-lived partnership with Howard Hughes, Sturges' career suffered a precipitous decline. His three subsequent Hollywood films were remote from the tastes of their time, and during his long exile in the 50s, his one realized European project, the bilingual Les Carnets du Major Thompson, was unsuccessful. His present reputation is that of a period director who ultimately lost contact with his audience. Even at the time of his greatest success, he was overshadowed by the emotions aroused by the war and the stylistic revolution introduced with Citizen Kane. He received an Academy Award for the script of The Great McGinty in 1940, and was nominated twice in 1944 for The Miracle at Morgan's Creek and Hail the Conquering Hero, though again as a writer rather than as a director.

His directorial style depended more on the pacing of action anc dialogue than on visual texture and composition. Sturges employed long uncut, 'single-take' scenes to establish the premises of his elabora *scripts, but when he shifted to slapstick, he often cut to reactions before the action had terminated. His instinct for timing comedy montage made his films the funniest of their era in terms of audience laughter. He was capable of cinematic licence with a talking horse, or a portrait that changed expressions. When he wanted to speed up the plot, he dispensed with dialogue and let the crisp movement and montage of silent farce fill the screen with hurtling bodies. In* Mad Wednesday, *he went so far as to begin with the last reel of Harold Lloyd's 1925 classic,* The Freshman, *after which he attempted to re-create Lloyd's vertiginous comedy effects with even wilder Sturges variations. As a screenwriter, he had pioneered in the development of the intricate flashback with* The Power and the Glory *in 1933, and his directed scenarios remain models of structural complexity.* – A. S.

My deepest critical instincts urge me to minimize the fact that I interviewed Preston Sturges in the summer of 1957. Why? Because, I suppose, I believe less than ever in the truth of direct personal confrontations between the artist and the critic. All directors, even the great ones, are human beings, but they are also something more or something less, or perhaps even something else. The link between artistry and psychology is still a tenuous one for me, and traits of character, common to millions of otherwise miscellaneous individuals, consequently seem as relevant as the signs of the zodiac. (Not that I have failed to explore the astrological potentialities of my subject, but the director's thoughtlessness in being born under the sign of the Virgin rather than the adjacent sign of the Lion discouraged this line of inquiry.) I must admit that Preston Sturges looked every inch a director. His eyes still retained their thoughtful glitter, and the greyness of his fifty-nine years was more an imperial grey than a sparrow grey. However, I already knew he was a director, and so how could I truthfully read the tea-leaves of character analysis? Unfortunately, what is adjudged fraudulent for a gipsy fortune teller is deemed valid for the professional investigator of the artist's mystery. It is hardly a secret that an experienced interviewer can usually mould a personality to specifications by asking the right questions, and most film directors are malleable enough to justify all sorts of preconceptions about their work. Of course, there is a grain of truth even in the lies inevitably elicited by inquisitors who know the answers before they ask the questions.

The point is that I do not wish to imply that my having met Preston Sturges confers any special authority upon my theory about his career. Nor do I believe that people who knew him intimately are any better qualified to evaluate his art than those who merely inspected his works. The conversational one-upmanship of personal intimacy seldom yields any original insight, particularly when the speaker assumes that an ounce of personal contact, however frivolous, is worth a ton of critical analysis, however dedicated. Strangely, although I have always believed in some version of the *auteur* theory, I find the cinema a particularly treacherous field for those who would establish a correlation between the personality of the artist as evidenced in his art and the personality of the same artist as displayed in a cocktail lounge or hotel suite. I am not arguing that such a correlation cannot be established, but only that I find my feeble powers of perception unequal to the task.

Anyway, to return to the summer of 1957, Preston Sturges was visiting New York to publicize what turned out to be his last film: *Les Carnets du Major Thompson*. On a hot Sunday afternoon in July or August, I have forgotten which, I arrived at the Algonquin where Sturges always registered when he was in New York. (He died at the Algonquin in 1959, but for a creature of habit this is fact, not irony.) A note at the desk suggested that the location of the interview be shifted to the more opulent surroundings of the St Regis where the director was comforting an ailing pasha of the Paramount front office. (I gathered subsequently that the hospitable pasha was one of the director's few remaining friends from the palmier days in Hollywood.) The atmosphere was relaxed, the Scotch refreshing, and the director-critic relationship properly respectful on my part. We talked for about six hours, most of the time off the record, and much of the time off the subject. The setting may have been too sybaritic at the St Regis, which is as much a producer's hotel as the Algonquin is a director's hotel. In the twilight of the afternoon, Lester Cowan burst in on us to watch an extra-inning baseball game on television. (Note: Sturges was not interested in baseball. Does that make his work less American?)

As I look back over my copiously misleading notes on the interview, I recall that I was vaguely guilty about the situation. Fortunately, I had not yet seen *Les Carnets du Major Thompson*, but even without this adverse information, I had the feeling that Sturges was a burnt-out talent. By the time I finally caught his last film, I saw no point in publishing the interview. It was too late for Sturges to make a comeback, but it was still too early, I felt, to treat him as a shrine. I could have spared myself these pompous rationalizations. Preston Sturges had played the hectic American game of success to the last card, but he had drawn a bilingual deuce. *Les Carnets du Major Thompson* is the kind of bad film which withers an enthusiast's soul. What hope is ther when a comedy director loses his rhythm and timing to the extent that he is less funny than his material? At this point in one's ruminations, the time-honoured theory of decline comes galloping to the rescue. Sturges had simply lost whatever it was that once made him a good director, and that was that. Or was it?

I have always been puzzled by the apparent fact that comic directors 'decline' more rapidly and more frequently than do serious directors. If the terms 'comic' and 'serious' lack both semantic precision and the logical relationship of opposites, it cannot be helped. These admittedly vague designations are used to limit my conception of comedy/ha-ha rather than comedy/not tragedy. It can be argued that the ability to make an audience laugh has less to do with comedy than with humour, less with wit than with slapstick, less with character than with caricature, less with a personal vision of the world than with the technical, almost totalitarian, manipulation of an audience. It can also be argued that the decibel rating of collective laughter is an absurdly impermanent criterion of lasting value.

Yet, like it or not, respect it or not, Preston Sturges once had a gift for making audiences laugh, and then one day, this gift apparently deserted him. His period of maximum craftsmanship coincided with his period of maximum productivity. The co-ordinates are easy enough to chart. Eight films for Paramount (1940–44) represent the crest and then down into the three-film trough of the Hughes-Zanuck trauma (1945–49) from which Sturges never recovered in a decade of exile (1950–59). The classical simplicity of this chronology is unusual even for the allegedly heartless dynamics of Hollywood production. What Sturges understood in 1957, certainly better than many of his admirers did, was that he needed Hollywood more than Hollywood needed him. His best comedies had always been parasitic rather than creative, recherché rather than revolutionary, the art more of a gadfly than of a butterfly. Whereas Welles has been redeemed in exile by his amateurism, Sturges was destroyed in exile by his professionalism. Perhaps it is better for an artist to abandon his audience before his audience abandons him, particularly in the realm of comedy/ha-ha. After all, Capra reigned only between 1934 and 1939, almost concurrently with McCarey. Previously, Lubitsch and Clair had been in vogue from about the mid-20s to the early 30s. As for the late James Agee's 'Golden Age of Comedy', who knows how long it would have lasted even without the advent of sound? By 1925, for example, Mack Sennett was viewed as an antiquated primitive. Even Chaplin was considered in decline from 1935 as far as risibility was concerned.

In most instances, the vogue for a personal comic style seems to fade

Hail the Conquering Hero: Eddie Bracken

with time and age. The older a director becomes, the less likely he is to be funny. As his audience turns to new approaches, the traditional director has a difficult choice. He can either change his style and thus sacrifice his personality, or he can maintain his style and thus lose his audience. Very often, the less personality a director has, the longer he will survive. Delbert Mann, for example, is presently a 'hot' director because his lack of style serves as a *tabula rasa* for any fashionable writer who comes along. Somehow Paddy Chayevsky, Terence Rattigan and Stanley Shapiro have kept Delbert Mann's feeble talent afloat for nearly a decade, during which time gifted directors have been sinking out of sight. On the other hand, Frank Capra and Leo McCarey have endeared themselves to the admirers of directorial continuity by becoming grotesquely anachronistic. Chaplin and Lubitsch ultimately attained something more than comedy/ha-ha, Clair and Wilder something less.

Yet, is not the comedy/ha-ha of yesterday ultimately the comedy, not tragedy of tomorrow? Do we ever really laugh at the past, or do we just acknowledge it with a nostalgic smile? Of course, time takes its toll of audiences as well as directors, and in this subjective jumble of time perspectives, we usually end reacting to comedy/ha-ha as an elusively individual experience which can only be discussed socially as comedy/not tragedy. In short, thinking about comedy is a very solemn enterprise.

Although clowns supposedly yearn to play Hamlet, they usually end up playing Lear. This is as true in the circus, the music hall, and the night club as it is in the cinema. The enjoyment of an old entertainer is often transformed into a stirring ritual of recognition. The entertainer appears and repeats a routine he has performed before and will perform again through all eternity. The time is long past for shocks and surprises. The entertainer and his audience engage in a conspiracy to hold back the clock for a few minutes or a few hours. George Jean Nathan once observed that drama critics, as a tribe, were moved more by the death of a bawdy clown than by the demise of a noble tragedian. Consequently, however high or low I might ever choose to rank Preston Sturges, the affection I have always felt for his best films would probably remain constant. The response of laughter imprisoned in a particular time and place gives Sturges a permanent retrospective value for those who want to remember the time and place, but a full appreciation of Sturges demands a full appreciation of Hollywood as well. Even though he seemed at times to be moving against the current, his films were never completely out of the stream.

What distinguishes Sturges from his contemporaries is the density and congestion of his comedies. The Breughel of American comedy directors, Sturges created a world of peripheral professionals – politicians, gangsters, executives, bartenders, cab drivers, secretaries, bookies, card sharps, movie producers, doctors, dentists, bodyguards, butlers, inventors, millionaires and derelicts. These were not the usual flotsam and jetsam of Hollywood cinema, but self-expressive cameos of aggressive individualism. With the determinism of the Sturges plots, these infinitely detailed miniatures served as contingent elements, and it is these elements, and the single-take, multiple viewpoint sequences formally demanded by these elements, which establish the comedies of Preston Sturges once and for all as comedy/not tragedy.

For the record, Sturges told me that the 'most perfect' film he had ever seen was Josef von Sternberg's *The Last Command*. He also admired Pierre Fresnay in *Monsieur Vincent*, but, like most directors, Sturges did not go to movies very often. Of his own films, he felt that *Hail the Conquering Hero* had 'less wrong with it' than any of his other films. The producers wanted to remove Ella Raines after the first rushes of *Hero*, but Sturges refused to consider a substitute. He was still scornful of Paramount for humiliating Vera Zorina in *For Whom the Bell Tolls* by replacing her with Ingrid Bergman after the hapless dancer had cut her hair for the part of Maria.

That night Preston Sturges appeared on the Mike Wallace Show, a television inquisition of that epoch. Sturges repudiated Rudy Vallee's 'sympathetic' tribute to him. Earlier that afternoon, I had gathered that Sturges was not happy with the heart-warming anecdotes Eddie Bracken's press agents were spreading in the columns about Eddie's charity to the director who had made him a star. It was the kind of acid scenario that Sturges might have written in the days of *Sullivan's Travels*, but this time there was no happy ending. Paris and New York were not Hollywood.

Preston Sturges: films as director

1940: *The Great McGinty*, *Christmas in July*
1941: *The Lady Eve, Sullivan's Travels*
1942: *The Palm Beach Story*
1944: *The Miracle at Morgan's Creek*, *Hail the Conquering Hero*, *The Great Moment*
1947: *Mad Wednesday*
1948: *Unfaithfully Yours*
1949: *The Beautiful Blonde from Bashful Bend*
1955: *Les Carnets du Major Thompson*

Part Two: Fugitives

John Huston in Preminger's *The Cardinal*

John Huston
talking to Gideon Bachmann, 1965

John Huston, son of the late Walter Huston, is one of the best known directorial personalities in the world. He projects his personality off screen as adeptly as he does on. Two of his productions, The Red Badge of Courage *and* The Misfits, *have inspired books about the productions themselves. Huston's image as an irascible individualist has been aided in no small measure by his publicized feuds with such famous producers as L. B. Mayer, David O. Selznick, and Darryl F. Zanuck. Huston's films reflect a masculine style clouded by a pessimistic outlook.* The Maltese Falcon, *his first feature film, is regarded by many critics as the best detective movie ever made. During the Second World War he made such distinguished documentaries as* Report from the Aleutians, The Battle of San Pietro, *and* Let There Be Light. *Since the war he has gained further prestige with* The Treasure of Sierra Madre, The Asphalt Jungle, *and* The African Queen. *On the whole, however, Huston's career since the war has raised disturbing questions about freedom and discipline in the cinema. That is to say, that in a quarter of a century of alleged liberation, John Huston has progressed from* The Maltese Falcon *to* The Bible. – A. S.

Meeting John Huston in Rome, where he was shooting The Bible, *turned out to be easier than meeting any other director I had ever interviewed. The day after I moved into a new apartment in Rome, people began calling me on the phone and asking for Huston. It turned out that I had accidentally moved into the apartment that he had vacated when he went to Egypt to shoot exteriors. I called up the studio and said I had some messages for Mr Huston. He invited me out to the set to watch him shoot the sequence of Noah's Ark.*

The De Laurentiis studios are the biggest in Europe today, and they are brand new. When I got there, I found myself in the centre of a circus – a typical travelling circus with caravans and cage carts, with animal noises and smells all around, and with a whole stationary zoo that had been constructed near the studios to supply the two hundred land animals and a thousand birds that were participating in the shooting of the ark sequence. The ark itself was inescapable – it wasn't just there once, but five times, in various sizes and in various stages of completion. Huston – who had less time than Noah – needed five arks to shoot the various stages of development of the vessel and in order to be able to shoot interiors or exteriors at will in any kind of weather.

Our actual meeting took place at the enclosure of the hippopotamus. Huston himself plays Noah in this sequence, and he was busy trying to convince the hippo to follow the requirements of the script. For an entire morning, while the cameras turned, the lights blazed, and Huston in his sackcloth costume endlessly repeated his biblical words, the animal refused to co-operate. Finally, in exasperation, Huston said to me: 'Let's give the poor beast a rest. What was it you wanted to talk to me about?'

And so right there, among the giraffes and the peacocks, the lions and the Himalayan goats, I asked Huston how he made films.

BACHMANN: *I think this is one of those rare times when I can start an interview [for radio use also] without any introductions. You're the kind of person who creates around him not only the normal fame as a director of the kind of films everybody has seen, but also a kind of personal aura, a sort of romantic halo, which means that you are as known as your work, and I don't have to go into a lot of explicatory remarks. And in any case, all I am interested in at this time is how you make films.*

HUSTON: I wish you had a better reason for omitting the introductions. On the other hand I am really happy that you go straight to the heart of the matter. This also corresponds to my method of working – it never seems to me that my films start with much preparation. In fact, I often get the feeling that my films make themselves. By this I don't mean that I don't take part in the production process, but very often I couldn't tell you exactly how ideas start to crystallize. For example, I never start off by saying 'I'm going to make a specific film', but some idea, some novel, some play suggests itself – very often it's something I read twenty-five or thirty years ago, or when I was a child, and have played around with in my thoughts for a long time. That was the case with pictures like *Moby Dick*, *The Red Badge of Courage*, and several others. Suddenly, surprisingly, I discover that I am actually making it. There's a film that I am going to make after I finish *The Bible* that has the same background: *The Man Who Would Be King*, the Kipling story. The first script on this film was written about ten years ago, but it was based on my reading of the story at age twelve or fifteen, and my impressions of it, that have remained with me. Most of the time my pictures begin with this kind of inbred idea, something that lives in me from long ago. Sometimes it's more erratic, though; someone has a picture they want you to make and if you think it's good enough to take a shot at, you step in as a sort of surgeon or practitioner. The only safe thing I can say is that there are no rules.

How does the script get written? Do you do it alone? And how long does it take you?

Again, there are no rules. I've written scripts and made pictures out of them in two weeks. At other times I've worked a year and a half just on a script. *The Maltese Falcon* was done in a very short time, because it was based on a very fine book and there was very little for me to invent. It was a matter of sticking to the ideas of the book, of making a film out of a book. On *Treasure of Sierra Madre*, I wrote the script in about three to four months, but I had had quite a long time to think about it before. The actual making of the film didn't take very long, but I had had the idea of making it since before the war. It was the first film I made after the war.

You wrote that one alone, and got an Oscar for writing it. But don't you sometimes write together with other people? Or, when other people write for you, do you take a very active part or do you leave them pretty much alone?

When I do not write alone – and of course you must remember that I began my film career as a writer, not as a director – I work very closely with the writer. Almost always I share in the writing. The writer will do a scene and then I'll work it over, or I'll write a scene and then the other writer will make adjustments later. Often we trade scenes back and forth until we're both satisfied.

You don't like to work with more than one other writer?

Not really. But sometimes other people make additions. For example, the writer of a play or a book on which I am basing a film. Tennessee Williams, for example, came and worked with Anthony Veiller and myself on the script for *Night of the Iguana*. He didn't come there to write, but once he was there he did do some writing, and actually he did some rather important writing for the film. But such cases are the exception.

Could you put into words some principles you employ in order to put ideas into film form? Do you feel there are any rules a writer for the cinema must follow?

Each idea calls for a different treatment, really. I am not aware of any ready formula, except the obvious one that films fall into a certain number of scenes, and that you have to pay attention to certain limitations that have to do with time, according to subject. Depending on what you are writing about, you have to decide the time balance between words and action. It seems to me, for example, that the word contains as much action as a purely visual scene, and that dialogue should have as much action in it as physical motion. The sense of activity that your audience gets is derived equally from what they see and from what they hear. The fascination, the attention of the man who looks at what you have put together, must be for the thoughts as much as for the happenings in your film. In fact, when I write I can't really separate the words from the actions. The final action – the combined activity of the film, the sum of the words and the visuals – is really going on only in the mind of the beholder. So in writing I have to convey a sense of overall progression with all the means at my command: words and images and sounds and everything else that makes film.

This brings up one of the basic questions about films that adapt literary works: in a book there are many things that you can't see or hear, but which in reading you translate directly into your own interior images and feelings. Emotions that are created in you neither through dialogue nor action. How do you get these into film? The monologues from Moby Dick, *for example?*

Well, first of all, I try to beware of literal transfers to film of what a writer has created initially for a different form. Instead I try to penetrate first to the basic idea of the book or the play, and then work with those ideas in cinematic terms. For example, to see what Melville wanted to say in the dialogue, what emotions he wanted to convey. I always thought *Moby Dick* was a great blasphemy. Here was a man who shook his fist at God. The thematic line in *Moby Dick* seemed to me, always, to have been: who's to judge when the judge himself is dragged before the bar? Who's to condemn, but he, Ahab! This was, to me, the point at which I tried to aim the whole picture, because I think that's what Melville was essentially concerned with, and this is, at the same time, the point that makes *Moby Dick* so extremely timely in our age. And if I may be allowed the side-observation: I don't think any of the critics who wrote about the film ever mentioned this.

I suppose you are speaking about the problem of taking personal responsibility in an age where the group has largely attempted to make decisions for the individual. This is an interpretation of Melville, or perhaps I should say one interpretation of Melville. And so in the attempt to understand the basic idea of a work (in order to translate those ideas into film) you are really doing more than that: you add your own interpretation, you don't just put into images what the original author wanted to say.

I don't think we can avoid interpretation. Even just pointing a camera at a certain reality means an interpretation of that reality. By the same token, I don't *seek* to interpret, to put my own stamp on the material. I try to be as faithful to the original material as I can. This applies equally to Melville as it applies to the Bible, for example. In fact, it's the fascination that I feel for the original that makes me want to make it into a film.

What about original material, where you are not adapting a play or a book? Are there any ideas of yours, basic ideas, which you try to express in your work? Do you feel that there is a continuity in your work in terms of a consistent ideology? In short, do you feel you are trying to say something coherent to mankind?

There probably is. I am not consciously aware of anything. But even the choice of material indicates a preference, a turn of mind. You could draw a portrait of a mind through that mind's preferences.

Well, let me do that for a minute, and see if what I see as a unifying idea in your work is indeed a coherent feeling on your part. I see that in your films there is always a man pitched against odds, an individual who seeks to retain a sense of his own individuality in the face of a culture that surrounds and tends to submerge him. I would call the style of your films the style of the frontier, or what the frontier has come to symbolize in American culture: a sense of rebellion against being put into a system, into a form of life and into a mode of thinking rigidly decided by others.

Yes, I think there is something there. I do come from a frontier background. My people were that. And I always feel constrained in the presence of too many rules, severe rules; they distress me. I like

Moby Dick

the sense of freedom. I don't particularly seek that ultimate freedom of the anarchist, but I'm impatient of rules that result from prejudice.

In any case, you believe that at the basis of every film of yours there is a basic idea, whether an idea of yours or one of another author. But how do you proceed to put that idea into film form? In writing, what do you do first, for example?

I don't envisage the whole thing at the beginning. I go a little bit at a time, always asking myself whether I am on the track of the basic thought. Within that, I try to make each scene as good as I can. This applies both to the writing and to the directing – to the whole process of preparation and production, in fact – which are only extensions of the process of writing. It's hard to break down into details.

Do you mean to say that you do not write the whole script in the beginning?

Oh yes, oh sure. I am speaking about the making of the film. I try to make it in sequence as much as possible, to develop the making of the film alone with the development of the story within the film. I try, for example, to give my actors a sense of development not only within the troupe, but also a sense of development within the story of the film. And I improvise if necessary. This is not a luxury; when one shoots as much on location as I do, improvisation is a necessity. Everything that happens in the process of making the film can contribute to the development of that film's story. But of course one always tries to remain within the bounds of the controllable as much as one can, to stay within the bounds of the script. But one must be open to take advantage of the terrain, of the things that the setting can give you.

Do you write your scripts with the idea of change and improvisation already in mind?

Improvisation is used more today than it used to be. Partly this is caused by a new, less rigid approach to film-making, and also partly by the decentralization of the production process. Actors have become producers, they have commitments of conflicting sorts, and it is no longer possible to prepare a script in great detail in a major studio set-up, and then call in your contract actors, whose time you control completely, and make the film in exact accordance to plan. It has simply become essential today to be more flexible, to adjust to new conditions, both practical and aesthetic.

Do you see this as a positive or a negative development?

It has certainly helped some directors to come into their own, people who could never have succeeded under the old, less independent system. Some French and Italian directors – Fellini in the vanguard – have found it possible to tell much more subjective stories, often their own, in a valid cinematographic way. Like *Otto e mezzo* for example.

What is the technical process of your script-writing?

Usually I write in longhand first, and then dictate a later version. I use a standard script form: action on the left and dialogue on the right. When it's finished it's mimeographed and distributed to the people who need to see it. I often change again later. Sometimes I finish the final version on the set itself, or change again something I've written as a final version the day before. Mostly these changes come to me when I hear the words first spoken by an actor. It's always different once it comes out of a living person's mouth. By this I do not mean that I try to adjust to an actor's personality – I try to do that as little as possible. When I write, I don't have in mind an actor, but a character. I don't conceive this character with a specific star in my mind. I guess what I am trying to do with this constant changing, is to try to put to work more than my own imagination, or at least allow my imagination the liberty of play, the liberty of coming out of its cage – which is me, my body, when I am alone and writing – and in this way it begins to live and to flower and gives me better service than when I put it to work abstractly, alone, in a room with paper and pencil, without the living presence of the material. Then, when the character has been born out of this extended imagination, I have to look for someone to play the role, and this someone isn't always necessarily the person whom I thought could play it originally, because often it no longer is the same character. In fact, I've often – at least, sometimes – delayed the making of a film because I couldn't find anybody to play the new and adjusted character that I had finally arrived at construing. Although in my experience you usually find someone; there are enough good actors if you are willing to wait a little.

Is it possible for you to tell how much of your writing comes from inside you, at the start, and how much is written in adjustment to a situation or to hearing your words spoken? And do you also adjust to location, for example? I mean, when you write about Sodom, do you write for Vesuvius, for the landscape where you decided to shoot those sequences?

It's the same thing as trying to interpret Melville. You write for an ideal. Then when you make the film, you try to live up to that ideal. Casting, locating, shooting: you try to stick to what you start with. Sometimes there are problems when the material changes in my hands, sometimes I have even miscast my own films. But generally these adjustment problems can be overcome. I've been pretty lucky that way. In fact, I can usually do pretty much exactly what I set out to do. I've been lucky.

Is that what gives you this tremendous peace that you seem to have on the set? I have watched perhaps a hundred directors shooting, and nobody is as calm. And you have this kooky set: this silly ark with all these animals, peacocks flying among the long necks of giraffes, hippos who refuse to act the scenes written for them, a hundred breakdowns a day with technical things caused by the animals, and you just stride through the whole thing in your Noah costume, feeding the giraffes, smiling and taking it easy . . .

I am astonished myself. And I marvel at the patience of everybody, especially the animals, who are among the best actors I've ever worked with. . . .

All typecast, too. . . . But, is that an answer?

In a way, yes. You see, in working with actors, I try to direct as little as possible. The more one directs, the more there is a tendency to monotony. If one is telling each person what to do, one ends up with a host of little replicas of oneself. So, when I start a scene, I always let the actor show me for the start how he imagines the scene himself. This applies not only to actors; as I tried to indicate before, I try to let the whole thing work on me, show me. The actors, the set, the location, the sounds, all help to show me what the correct movement could be. So what I said about the animals wasn't only a joke. Because, you see, the animals have one great advantage as actors: they know exactly what they want to do, no self-doubts, no hesitations. If you watch them, quite extraordinary opportunities present themselves, but you must see them. Here in the Noah's Ark sequence of *The Bible* this has happened a number of times. Animals do remarkable things. The hippo opened his mouth and let me pet him inside.

Is that when you wrote the line, which you say to Noah's wife at that point: 'There is no evil in him, wife. Do not fear him!'

Exactly. And very fine actors are as much themselves as animals are. I would rather have someone whose personality lends itself to the role than a good actor who can simulate the illusion of being the character. I do not like to see the mechanics of acting. The best you can get, of course, is when the personality lends itself exquisitely to the part and when that personality has the added attribute of being technically a fine actor so he can control his performance. That is the ideal.

What do you consider to be the attributes of a fine actor?

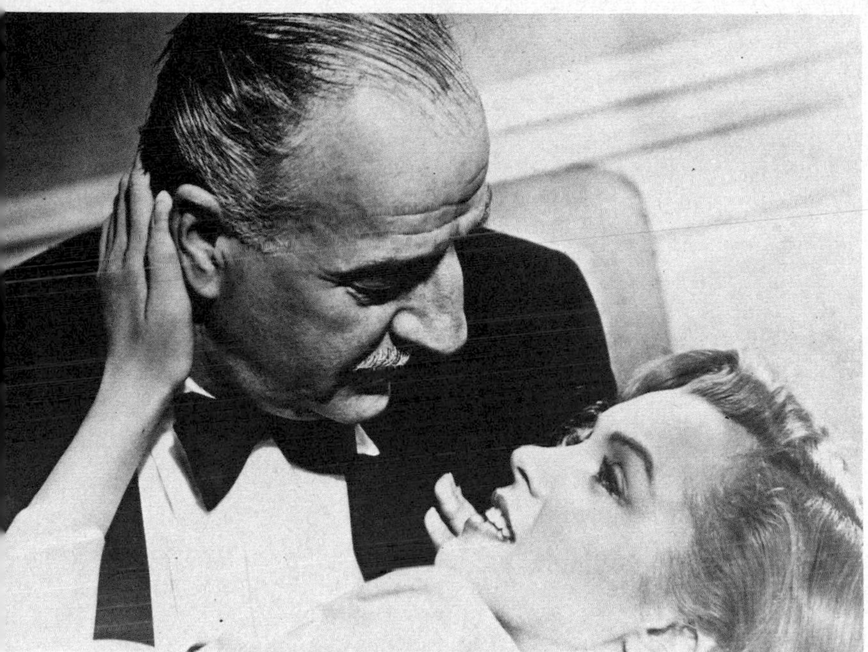

The Asphalt Jungle: Louis Calhern, Marilyn Monroe

The shading he can give a line, his timing, his control, his knowledge of the camera, his relationship to the camera – of course, I'm talking about film acting.

What should an actor's relationship to the camera be?

He must have an awareness of the size of his gesture, his motion, in relation to the size that his image will be on the screen. It isn't absolutely an essential quality, but it is very useful. I don't mean that I tell him the focal length of the lens I'm using and expect him to adapt himself accordingly, but a good actor has an almost instinctual awareness of these things. When an actor comes from the stage, he usually has to make adjustments of this kind. He doesn't need to project, he doesn't need to make his voice heard over a distance. He can speak very quietly. He can be more economical in every way before the camera than he could be on stage. And he can work with the small details of his face.

Does a good actor, one with all the best technical attributes, make a star?

Oh, no. One doesn't have much to do with the other. Of course, the star must know how to act, and a good actor can become a star, but what a star really is, is hard to describe. There are many fine and beautiful actors who would never be stars. I don't think that's a lack in their personalities, because it's beyond that – something very mysterious happens. Some personalities seem to take on another dimension on the screen. They become bigger than life. When that happens, there is a star. Some stars are not good actors, but a lot of good actors aren't stars.

Can you recognize this star quality when you meet a person, or do you have to see the person on the screen first?

I recognize it more or less. For instance, I had Marilyn Monroe in her first real film role [in *The Asphalt Jungle*] and I can't claim to have had any notion of where she was headed, but I could feel that she was going to be good in this film and I chose her over a number of others. But still I didn't dream of the places she would go.

How did you meet her?

She was brought in by an agent in Hollywood.

Did you have one of those ideal characters ready in mind when you saw her?

Yes, and she was it. I guess it was an interesting moment, but I didn't know it at the time.

How do you – even more or less – recognize the star quality?

In certain instances, it stands out all over the individual, just as it stands out in certain horses now and then. You look at an animal and you know it is top class. It's the same with certain persons – with an Ava Gardner, with a Humphrey Bogart, with a Katharine Hepburn. There's no mistaking that quality when you see it any more than there is a chance of mistaking the looks of a great horse in the paddock. It's hard to put in other words, and it varies from person to person.

In any case, you are speaking of something that isn't just a flamboyance of bearing?

On the contrary. Flamboyance is something that people assume when they feel a lack of structure in their own characters. But this, too, is not invariably the case. I've known some flamboyant people who were extraordinary too. Flamboyance is all right when it is a natural expression of something that is really that person. It's like every other characteristic that a person has: it's good only if it's real. I don't like it if people put on false surfaces, and I think by now I can tell when they do. And it always works against my choosing a certain person to play in a film.

Let's see if we can follow your film-making method through logically and go on to a description of the process of turning the script into film.

Actually I don't separate the elements of film-making in such an abstract manner. For example, the directing of a film, to me, is simply an extension of the process of writing. It's the process of rendering the thing you have written. You're still writing when you're directing. Of course you're not composing words, but a gesture, the way you make somebody raise his eyes or shake his head is also writing for films. Nor can I answer precisely what the relative importance, to me, of the various aspects of film-making is, I mean, whether I pay more attention to writing, directing, editing, or what-have-you. The most important element to me is always the idea that I'm trying to express, and everything technical is only a method to make the idea into clear form. I'm always working on the idea: whether I am writing, directing, choosing music or cutting. Everything must revert back to the idea; when it gets away from the idea it becomes a labyrinth of rococo. Occasionally one tends to forget the idea, but I have always had reason to regret this whenever it happened. Sometimes you fall in love with a shot, for example. Maybe it is a *tour de force* as a shot. This is one of the great dangers of directing: to let the camera take over. Audiences very often do not understand this danger, and it is not unusual that camera-work is appreciated in cases where it really has no business in the film, simply because it is decorative or in itself exhibitionistic. I would say that there are maybe half a dozen directors who really know their camera – how to move their camera. It's a pity that critics often do not appreciate this. On the other hand I think it's OK that audiences should not be aware of this. In fact, when the camera is in motion, in the best-directed scenes, the audiences should not be aware of what the camera is doing. They should be following the action and the road of the idea so closely that they shouldn't be aware of what's going on technically.

Am I right in assuming, then, that you do not share the modern view that the form of a film can be as important as its content? I take it, from what you say, that you are interested more in what is being said than in how it is being said.

When you become aware of *how* things are being said, you get separated from the idea. This doesn't mean that an original rendering isn't to be sought after, but that rendering must be so close to the idea itself that you aren't aware of it.

If the optimum is to stay close to the original idea without imposing one's individuality upon it, then the old Thalberg-Ince system of having a script written by one man and then farming it out to another to shoot, wouldn't appear to be so bad.

That's carrying a principle to an extreme. Let's be sure to have enough regard for *style*. I am not saying that the director who is carrying on to film the idea created by another man should obliterate his individuality. After all, there are many ways – as many as there are people – to do any one thing, including the direction of a film. One sticks to an idea within one's own ability and with the means that are native to oneself, and not through employing means that are so commonplace that anybody could use them. What goes for film also goes for literature, for any form of art; the originality of Joyce is in no way to be divorced from what he was saying. There's no separation between style and subject matter, between style and intention, between style and – again – the idea. I do not mean to indicate, in anything I say, that the work of a man shouldn't bear witness to the personality of that man, beyond the fact that he expresses a specific idea in that work. It's the combination of his personality and the idea he expresses which creates his style.

How do you define style?

As the adaptation of the word or the action to the idea. I remember when I was a kid this question of style puzzled me. I didn't know what they meant by the style of a certain writer. One day Plato's *Apology* fell into my hands. It was an accident, but it was an eye-opener for me as far as style was concerned. I understood that the words of Socrates were in keeping with the monumentality of his conceptions.

Do you adjust your style to what you consider the intelligence level of your public to be? In other words, if you made a film today about Socrates in the style of Socrates (if I may oversimplify for a moment), this style itself would stand between the ideas you are trying to express and the person in some small town who might see your film.

I don't adjust to what they call the level of the audience. The mentality of an audience is something I consider as quite extraordinary. Audiences can feel and think with a celerity and a unison perhaps beyond the power of its most intelligent members. They laugh instantly if something is funny, and in other ways, too, they react in the most extraordinarily perceptive way. So I think it's nonsense to listen to producers who tell you 'they won't understand you'. When I make a picture I go under the assumption that if I like something, there are enough people like me who will like it too, to make it worth doing.

Does that mean that to make something worthwhile it must be accepted by a major number of other people?

Yes, there's that requirement.

I mean, beyond the financial requirement that films be sold.

Well, you can't go beyond that.

I mean in terms of your own personal satisfaction. Is it very important to you that your films be seen by many people, and understood by many people?

I don't make pictures for myself. And I do believe that if I like a film, others will like it, too. I make films with the intention that they be seen. I make a picture for others. It's not just a personal satisfaction that I'm seeking. On the other hand I don't try to imagine the reactions or to figure out, ahead of time, the minds of others. It's hard enough for me to understand my own mind and to understand myself. I couldn't possibly speculate on what fifty million people might like or not like. I can only hope that among fifty million there are enough who resemble me in taste.

Do you think that a film is better if more people like it?

Sometimes. But this is quite a question that you've asked me there. We're getting into quite an abstract area. Films are not always immediately popular. Sometimes films acquire popularity slowly over the years, as has happened with some of mine. For example *The Red Badge of Courage*. And also *Beat the Devil*, which was a complete bust when it came out, and now it has a sort of cult following. Over the years these two pictures have probably had bigger audiences than *Moulin Rouge*, which was immediately successful.

Let's get back to the film-making process. You've assembled, changed, and rewritten your script and chosen your actors. Do you give them the script to read before they come on the set?

Yes, of course. They read the script before they ever get any instructions from me. Sometimes they then like to talk about the role before they appear on the set in make-up. But I try to tell them as little as possible, because I want to see what they can give me. There's always time later to give them what I've thought about. In the beginning I want them not to be influenced by my predeterminations, because that would close up their individual creativity, it would eliminate their ability to give me something new, something I might not have thought of myself. The best illustration of this is the story of my first film, the first one I directed. I made drawings. I wanted to be very sure. I was uncertain of myself as far as the camera was concerned and I wanted to be sure not to fumble, not to get lost in the mechanical aspects of the film. So I made drawings of every set-up, but didn't show the drawings to anyone. I discovered that about 50 per cent of the time the actors themselves automatically fell into the drawings, and about 25 per cent of the time I had to pull them into the drawings, which were, in fact, set-up designs. But another 25 per cent of the time they did something better than I had thought of myself.

That means you work through the actor's intellectual comprehension of your material?

Of course, and I benefit from this comprehension very often. In fact, even before Stanislavski I think actors always functioned this way. The only reason it became such a fad was that so many young people were marching out on to the screen without any preparation, so suddenly the emphasis shifted strongly towards preparation and it was made into something of a religion; I mean 'the method' and the Actors' Studio, etc. And of course many good actors came out of that school. Personally I don't prefer conscious actors, or actors with that particular training, nor do I reject them, because I believe that every good actor prepares, maybe not always so consciously.

Do you let them rehearse a lot on the set?

It depends on the scene. I don't let them rehearse too much, as a rule, but some scenes call for more rehearsal than others.

What kind of instructions are you likely to give an actor?

Anything that will give him a sense of security. In the initial conversations, I may talk about the idea of the role, what its relation to the whole picture is, the background of the character. Some actors like to talk a lot. It helps them.

Do you yourself like to talk a lot?

Not very much. But I find it my job to do anything I can to help the actor, to make him feel at ease, to give him a sense of independence, of importance, if you will. I'll do anything for this, even talk. But I always keep hoping that it will be the actor who will show me, rather than the other way round.

What then do you tell them, in precise terms, when they get on the set? Do you tell them where to stand . . . ?

Not even that. I let them stand where they please. Sometimes they wait to be told, and I always try to get them to take the reins themselves. I say, let's rehearse the scene, you show me. Mostly they do this of their own accord. I'd say four out of five times the actors – especially if they are very good actors – take over right away. I don't have to say a word. If they are talented and intelligent they expect to be let alone. For example, working with George Scott, I seldom even gave a clue of direction, and he did exactly what I wanted without any of us ever saying a word, practically. Only occasionally I would have to ask him to move a bit to the left or the right. His approach to the scene would be so real and true that I couldn't add anything, except those mechanical camera directions. Not all actors are that good, and some you have to work a lot with. Sometimes very good actors need a lot of direction, too, but if they are gifted and intelligent one is on the same wavelength anyway and one can talk in a kind of code. They catch immediately what you want, and they fit right in. They catch what you want, use it, and it comes back to you stronger, better than you gave it to them, because they have digested it and are using their talents to put it into reality. Sometimes I have directed people in ways which disappointed me, and have later discovered that when I left them alone to do what they wanted, it came out better. I suppose it's because a good actor knows what he can do well and how, and through this self-knowledge he can produce something I couldn't abstractly imagine. Sometimes I shoot a scene both ways: mine and his, and often – like for example with Clark Gable – I find that his version is better on the screen.

Do you consider the actor raw material for your manipulation or an alive organism that you must adjust to? Does he retain his personality in what you make him do or is he only a means to your end?

He's a means to my end only insofar as he retains his personality.

You try not to impose yourself on him at all?

I try not to. He must be a very bad actor for me to try to do this. And, by the way, on the part of the director there is as much work in concealing bad performances as there is in developing good ones.

What else, besides controlling the actors, does your job of directing include? How much control do you exercise over the camera, the light, the sets, the other mechanics?

Lighting is almost completely up to the cameraman, who of course must be in complete sympathy with the director. The set-up is something else. There you're telling the story, the composition will appear on the screen, also the movement of the camera. The variety of material to be included in the shot, and its displacement, those are things I try to control. Again, when I decide about these things, I go by the rules that are imposed upon me by the central idea, by what I'm trying to say, and how I've decided to say it. And I choose set-ups and camera angles that will tell my story as quickly and as strongly and as surely as possible.

Do you have the precise set-up in mind when you write the script?

No. I write first, then seek the set-up that demonstrates. And I find that if the set-up is chosen well, I hardly ever have to change a line for a set-up or a set-up for a line. The fact that I write the words first doesn't mean the words have precedence. I find that dialogue and camera set-up are not at war. I don't seek a set-up to carry a certain word; I seek a certain word and a certain set-up to carry a certain idea. Sometimes one single word is enough for this, or even complete silence, if the image is right.

Do you think the fewer words spoken in a film, the better film it is?

Depends on the film. Some films depend on words. Take *Night of the Iguana*. Take the spoken words out of that, and you won't have very much.

Is that only because that particular script was based on a play? Or do you feel that scripts that are very word-oriented could also be read as literature as a play can?

I don't think you can make rules. In the case of *Iguana* the words were important because they carried Tennessee Williams's thoughts. But I think a good screenplay could be read as literature, too. It simply depends on the particular material.

You are not taking sides, then, in the perennial controversy over what's more important in film, the word or the image?

I don't see that they are in conflict. Depending on what is being said they complement each other in the hands of a good craftsman.

Well, there's a difference in impact, of course. I'm thinking of the aesthetic problems of the intake of stimuli by a man sitting in a dark hall. If you put words and images on the same level, certain problems arise. Sitting there in the dark, his ears can be unbusy for some length of time so you can introduce silences on the sound-track. But there's got to be something on the screen to see *all the time.*

The problem of the attention of the audience to the screen has occupied me quite a lot. Because of the dark tunnel in which he sits, the spectator in a film has nothing else to fix his attention on to, only that oblong of light which is the screen. This causes a whole different *time factor* to operate in his process of perception, than in other forms of spectacle, like plays. Two or three seconds of delay in a scene in a film can immediately cause a dull and laborious effect, and the viewer can begin to behold himself, rather than the screen. He shifts in his seat and coughs and scratches and feel his internal organs at work. So you must work to this different time factor when directing a film. Film isn't like most arts, where you can stop watching for a while – you can put a book aside, stop watching a wall with pictures while taking a cup of coffee – but in film all the viewer can do is watch, watch constantly, and the film-maker has to fill the screen for him all the time. It's a requirement of film-making that the viewer's attention be held all the time. It's a requirement, unfortunately, that's not often lived up to. I know of only very few instances in my own experience of film-going where this requirement was constantly being met. On the other hand, making films where something is constantly happening, also imposes greater demands on the viewer than is the case in any other medium. But there are many things inherent in the medium that work for you; the whole immediacy of the experience, and the subjectivity of the emotions that can derive from a good film. The ideal film, it seems to me, is when it's as though the projector were behind the beholder's eyes, and he throws on to the screen that which he *wants* to see. Films are usually very good for their first two or three minutes. The audience is completely taken outside of itself. They are not aware of themselves. And then comes that awful moment when they become self-aware once more. It's the film that allows this to happen, of course. I think that one of the problems of the people who make films is that they have not realized that most of the devices of film are inherent in the physiology of man. I mean, all the things we have laboriously learned to do with film, were already part of the daily physiological and psychological experience of man before film was invented, and if we only knew how to make a bridge between these natural experiences and that which we put on the screens, we would be able to eliminate those dead moments, those laborious times, when the human being begins to feel the distance between his real experience and that which is suggested to him via the screen. Let me make an experiment – maybe you will understand better what I mean. Move your eyes, quickly, from an object on one side of this room to an object on the other side. In a film you would use the cut. Watch! There – you did exactly what I expected: in moving your head from one side of the room to the other, you briefly closed your eyes. Try it again, in the other direction. There! You see, you do it automatically. Once you know the distance between the two objects, you blink instinctively. That's a cut. If you were to pan, as we could do with the camera or as you could do with your eyes, from one side to the other, passing all the objects on the way, and then back again, it would become tedious beyond endurance. This does it for you. In the same way, almost all the devices of film have a physiological counterpart. It's a matter of learning – again – to use it.

And you can look at most other filmic devices with this point of view. Take the dissolve. Your thoughts are changing. There's that moment of impingement of thoughts and images where you are aware of your surroundings, or perhaps looking at something else, outside your direct field of vision. Thoughts change while the things you see intermingle. And take the fade-out: that corresponds to sleep. It's an opportunity to rest, to change completely. Exactly as we use it in film.

I'm particularly intrigued by what you said about the time factor. Film is the only graphic medium in which the intake period, the time it takes to receive the stimulus, on the part of the spectator, is controlled not by that spectator, but by the maker of the film. You control how long he looks. In fact, it has always seemed to me that this possibility of controlling the time element is much more important, is a more basic aesthetic element in film, than the fact that it moves. Movement is simply one of the functions of time. Film is the only art form in which you can manipulate time. In fact, I would say one could make a film in which nothing moved, which would be composed entirely of stills, but which would still be entirely 'filmic' because it controls the psychological experience of time in an artificial way. Sometimes I wonder how many film-makers are aware of the power they possess through this capacity to change man's concepts of time.

Most film-makers are aware of the time element in the sense that they are worried about the lagging attention of the viewer. That means they are aware of the problem of time manipulation, but not consciously. They know they've got to speed up a scene, for example. They don't know why – they don't know what they're doing. But then I don't necessarily believe that complete consciousness makes better artists.

What other elements of film-making do you try to control as part of the creative process?

One of the most important elements is to control the producer. Artistically, I am most concerned with controlling the colour. Some films would suffer from being in colour. Colour, like camera acrobatics, can be a distraction unless it's functional in the film. But both are important, black-and-white and colour film. Artists have pigments, but they continue to draw. Certain subjects are better in one and others in the other medium. I would never have made *Freud* in colour. There was a certain projection of a unilateral thought, the development of a logic. Colour would only have distracted. I wanted the audience to follow the logic that was as real as a detective's pursuit of a criminal, without distraction by visual elements. And by the same token, I would never have made *Moulin Rouge* in black-and-white. And in *Moby Dick* I tried to combine both by inventing a technique of printing both types of film together.

Iuston as Noah

Do you always try to experiment with new ideas? Do you feel tha there is a continuity, in this sense, in your work?

As far as I can say, talking about myself, I think there is a certai uniformity in my work from the beginning up till now. And the on thing I always try to experiment with is accepting suggestions from th people who work with me. I don't like to dictate, I like to receiv stimuli from all: not only the cameraman and the actors, but the grip and the script girl, or the animal trainers as in the case of *The Bible*. try to create an atmosphere on the set where everyone feels they ca participate. I guess this is as much as I can say in terms of having basic theory of directing: letting the material have complete freedom and imposing myself only when necessary. That's what I meant whe I was guilty of that original cliché by remarking that I let my film make themselves.

How do you finish your films?

I shoot very economically, sometimes not enough, even. I shoot a if I were editing in the camera. Then there's usually only one way t cut the film. I look at the rushes every day, again allowing for m collaborators' views in choosing the final takes to use. Then, when th film is cut, I choose the music with the idea that it has to have dramatic purpose. I hate decorative music. I want the music to hel tell the story, illustrate the idea, not just to emphasize the images That means that it must have a certain autonomy. And there shoul be economy.

Would you say that your principle of making films, and your principl of using the various elements, like music, for example, is this economy

Everything must serve the idea – I must say this again and again The means used to convey the idea should be the simplest and the mos direct and clear. I don't believe in overdressing anything. Just what i required. No extra words, no extra images, no extra music. But i seems to me that this is a universal principle of art. To say as much a possible with a minimum of means. And to be always clear about wha you are trying to say. That means, of course, that you must know wha you are trying to say. So I guess my first principle is to understan myself, and then to find the simplest way to make others understan it, too.

John Huston: films as director

1941: *The Maltese Falcon*
1942: *In This Our Life, Across the Pacific*

943: *Report from the Aleutians* (documentary)
944: *The Battle of San Pietro* (documentary)
945: *Let There Be Light* (documentary)
948: *The Treasure of the Sierra Madre, Key Largo*
949: *We Were Strangers*
950: *The Asphalt Jungle*
951: *The Red Badge of Courage, The African Queen*
953: *Moulin Rouge*
954: *Beat the Devil*
956: *Moby Dick*
957: *Heaven Knows, Mr Allison*
958: *The Barbarian and the Geisha, The Roots of Heaven*
960: *The Unforgiven*
961: *The Misfits*
962: *Freud (Freud – the Secret Passion)*
963: *The List of Adrian Messenger*
964: *The Night of the Iguana*
966: *The Bible*
967: *Casino Royale* (co-director), *Reflections in a Golden Eye, Sinful Davy*
968: *The Madwoman of Chaillot* (taken over by Bryan Forbes)
969: *A Walk with Love and Death, The Kremlin Letter*

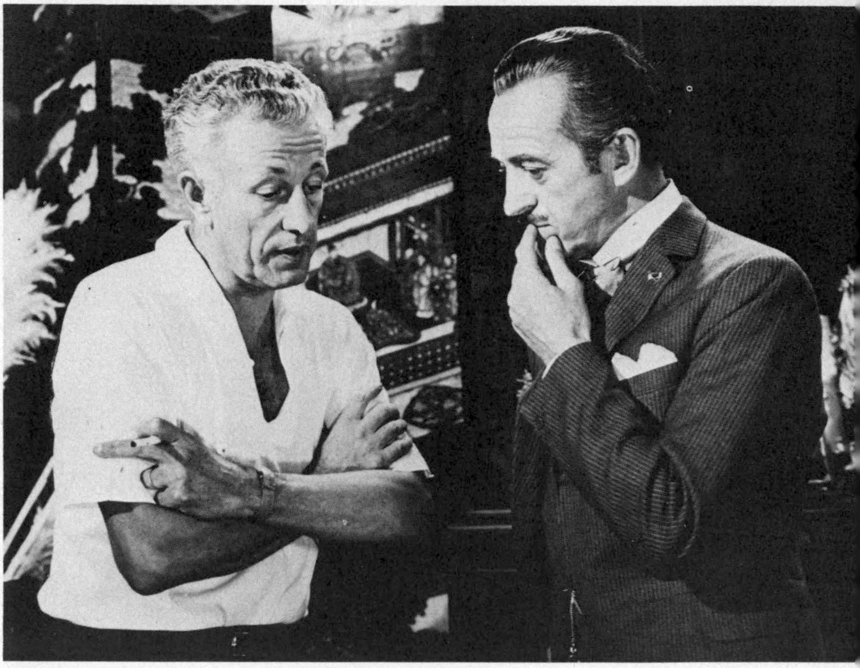

Nicholas Ray with David Niven on the set of *55 Days at Peking*; Joseph Losey during th production of *Accident*

Joseph Losey and Nicholas Ray alking to Penelope Houston and John Gillett, 1961

a Crosse, Wisconsin; population about 50,000; birthplace of Nicholas Ray and Joseph Losey. As an entry for a cinéaste's guide-book, this one must take a little beating. Add that they both went, if not quite simul-aneously, to the same school (Losey was born in January, 1909; Ray in August, 1911) and this is only the second link in the careers of two film-makers whom chance, and later the critics, seem determined to bracket ogether.

Ray was thirty-six when he made his first feature, They Live by Night*; Losey, at thirty-nine, followed him with* The Boy with Green Hair. *Both ictures were made for R.K.O.; but coincidence doesn't enter into it ere, since this was the time when Dore Schary was strenuously remind-ng R.K.O. that it was, after all, the studio that had let Welles make* Citizen Kane. *Both men arrived at the cinema via theatre and radio, Losey in particular having pursued a pyrotechnic course through the heatre of the 30s. He was writing book and theatre reviews in his early wenties, worked on some of the first stage shows at Radio City Music Hall, and after a tour of Scandinavia and Russia came back in 1936 to ut on the celebrated* Living Newspaper *productions, in which Nicholas Ray acted. He edged his way towards the cinema by way of a marionette* *film sponsored by the petroleum industry for the New York World's Fair followed by several educational shorts. In 1942 he was working in radio in 1945, after military service, he made an Oscar-winning short i M.G.M.'s* Crime Doesn't Pay *series. Then came the famous Hollywoo production of Brecht's* Galileo, *with Charles Laughton. Of his work wit Brecht, Losey has been quoted as saying: 'My own experience was tha he didn't follow his own theories too rigidly. When dealing with actors for instance, he used whatever means produced the best results. If th Stanislavsky method worked, that was fine; but he was always ready t try other approaches.'*

Nicholas Ray, meanwhile, had been a slower starter in the theatre though a precociously successful radio script, at the age of sixteen, ha won him a scholarship to study under Frank Lloyd Wright. In the theatr he worked with the producer John Houseman, went with him to the Offic of War Information, and in the early 40s was engaged on propagand radio programmes. In 1943 he directed Lute Song *on Broadway, wit Yul Brynner and Mary Martin; in 1946* Beggar's Song, *with Alfre Drake. Sandwiched between, however, had been a trip to Hollywood a assistant to Kazan on* A Tree Grows in Brooklyn. *He arrived in Holly wood as a feature director in 1947, shooting* They Live by Night *in brisk seven weeks. The producer was his old associate John Houseman who was also one of the men behind the production of* Galileo.

Ray made fourteen Hollywood films in ten years, working for most o the major companies. He came to Europe in 1957 for Bitter Victory, *wen back again for* Wind Across the Everglades *and* Party Girl, *the returned to Europe to make* The Savage Innocents *(shot at Pinewoo and elsewhere) and* King of Kings *(shot in Spain). Losey's caree meanwhile, had been abruptly checked after five American pictures. H was in Italy, working on a co-production variously known as* Strange on the Prowl *and* Encounter, *when he learnt that he had been calle before the Un-American Activities Committee. Threatened with black listing in Hollywood, he settled in England but at first could take n credit for the films he made here.* The Sleeping Tiger *and* The Intimat Stranger *were both made under pseudonyms.* Time Without Pity *(1956 broke the enforced silence; since then Losey has made four more Britis films, all correctly credited.*

Including pictures to be released later this autumn, Ray has no directed nineteen features and Losey thirteen. Both scored the same kin of critical success early on (Ray with They Live by Night, *Losey wit* The Dividing Line*); both then lost some ground with the critics, thoug Ray made a spectacular come-back with* Rebel Without a Cause*; an both now find themselves labelled as cult directors, a distinction hard t* *in and even harder to shake off.* Cahiers du Cinéma, *which has long dmired Ray, caught up with Losey only last year. The lead has been uickly followed, in Britain and elsewhere. M. Hoveyda says that* Party irl *gives him 'a glimpse of the kingdom of heaven'; Losey has been ompared, for reasons not immediately apparent, to Klee and Stravinsky. he game of critical cross-references is in full cry. Adulation can scarcely o further than the case of one over-eager French journalist who ontrived to publish an interview with Ray, without actually meeting m, in which he generously ascribed to his hero many of his own pinions.*

Something less than enthusiasm for the Ray-Losey cult, however, does ot imply lack of interest in the film-makers themselves. We hope, at ast, that we managed to communicate this to both Nicholas Ray and oseph Losey, when a group of us were able to talk with them, separately nd at length, last August. The interviews published here are based on ese conversations. – Penelope Houston and John Gillett [1961]

icholas Ray

icholas Ray is tall, eager, communicative, an improbably young-oking fifty. He speaks slowly, as though he were chipping his entences off some rough block of ideas, knocking his thoughts into ape as he goes. Talking about his own work, he is self-critical, bsorbed; he is concerned about what people think, concerned pecially about clarity, the way an idea communicates itself on the reen. Looking back recently at his early films, shown *en bloc* a few onths ago in Paris, he said he was disconcerted to find how often he peated himself, took pains to emphasize a point already clearly nough made. Talking to him, one feels the same pressure towards icidity, together with an undiminished fascination with the mechanics nd possibilities of his craft. His image of the cinema – 'the biggest, ost expensive electric train anyone could be given to play with' – is a oung enthusiast's.

As a film-maker with rather more experience than most of critical akes and ladders, Ray might be expected to be interested in what – r how – critics think. Clearly he is; and equally clearly he finds the xisting critic-director relationship rather less than ideal. He would ke greater definition of terms, would like the critic to set out the andards he applies in evaluating a film, then to meet the director on e ground of a specific picture which could be analysed by critic and irector according to their separate lights. This would be a fascinating boratory exercise, and one hopes it can be realized. A critic's ossible answer – that he knows what he's looking for on the screen when he finds it – is not as evasive as it might appear. Critical 'star dards' are set up to be knocked down by film-makers demanding ne responses. But Ray is right in pressing towards a firmer, sharpe definition of terms.

He's disturbed, in fact, by simple ignorance, the failure of so man reviewers to know basic technical facts of the thing they're writin about. One of us mentioned a reviewer's reference to 'slow cuts' as case in point: we knew what was meant, but the way it was pu revealed depths of disinterest. Talking of the French critics, Ra readily concedes that some of his admirers are 'pretty far out' in the wilder judgments. It was disconcerting, he said, to resee one of his ow films, to point out where he felt he had gone wrong, and to hear a around the murmurs of *formidable*, *merveilleux* from an audienc which would not admit the possibility of error. At the same time, h feels, the young French critics *do* know more. 'They make it the business to know.' And they have proved their point in action: on test of a critic is the sort of films he makes when he stops being a criti

Generally speaking, Ray clearly feels that critics are too resistant t innovation. (How many of us, for instance, would hold now to th opinions we first expressed about CinemaScope?) Screens, he say had to get bigger; and he regards *How the West Was Won*, the firs story film in Cinerama, as a test case, and perhaps also a test for th critics. Are we prejudiced, he asks, against size itself? We try to assur him, not perhaps successfully, that if very big films usually get un enthusiastic reviews it's not because of a critical resistance movemen but because they impose problems few film-makers have prove equipped to tackle. Ray himself likes to work in CinemaScop though not always. Pointing across to the high trees of Green Park, h commented that a story set there should never make a CinemaScop subject. He's also deeply interested in colour, and the cinema's failur to explore it imaginatively, to know how and what to select. He fel he said, that the black-and-white 35mm. picture had more or less ha its day, then saw Jean-Luc Godard's *Breathless* and slightly revised hi opinion.

He also liked Godard's Berlin Festival film *Une Femme est un Femme*: 'It's really inventive; it's got some bounce.' Not surprisin perhaps, that Ray should enjoy Godard's work, or that he shoul prefer Fellini's talent as a film-maker to Antonioni's, while willingl conceding his respect for Antonioni's quality of mind. *L'Avventura* h finds attenuated and fragile; *La Dolce Vita* he admires, though think ing the whole Steiner episode, from organ playing to suicide, much to predictable. He sees, he says, too few films – an almost universa omplaint among film-makers. But his admirations are firmly ositive: Buñuel, Jean Renoir, Bergman, and, from Hollywood, Billy /ilder.

Ray's capacity for self-criticism and appraisal goes well beyond nything usually encountered among directors. His best film, he feels, *Rebel Without a Cause* (most of us would probably agree); he has olid affection for *The Lusty Men*, a story about rodeo people, starring obert Mitchum and Susan Hayward, which has hardly been revived nce its first appearance in 1952, and a reminiscent interest, slightly nged with scepticism, about *In a Lonely Place*, his Hollywood urder story. Of his first film, *They Live by Night*, he said that he ddenly thought about it again a year or so ago, walking down a dark, raughty corridor in a house in Maine, and wished that he'd been able manage 'just one more angle in the car scene'. Otherwise, he felt it ot about as close as could be expected to what he wanted it to express. e's also satisfied with *Bigger Than Life*, with one major reservation. his was the story of a man who reached the edge of insanity after king cortisone; and Ray argues that he made a bad mistake in ctually naming the drug, involving his audience in the pros and cons one particular medical discussion, rather than letting the miracle-rug theme carry his point about the fallacy of believing in *any* magical olution to a human problem.

All these films have an element of violence, and there's no doubt at violence fascinates Ray as the unpredictable factor in human ersonality. He's equally concerned, though, with the precise placing a story, its degree of documentary truth. The rodeo world of *The usty Men*; the intelligent suburbia of *Bigger Than Life*; the Eskimo ttlement of *The Savage Innocents*; the gipsy life of *Hot Blood*: these veral settings he sees as a series of explorations. One of his early ms, *On Dangerous Ground* (1950, with Robert Ryan and Ida Lupino), as a not very successful attempt to link two kinds of violence – the utality of the hard city cop, confronted with the raw winter country-de which was the scene of murder. Some moments in cars (Ray, like ntonioni, has an eye for a car scene) and some snow-and-ice land-apes were about all we, or Ray, felt like recalling from the film. But emphasized that he had driven out with police squad cars in the ughest district of Boston for weeks before making it, just as he udied endless photographs of gipsy ceremonial before embarking on *ot Blood*.

Ray is absorbed by fact, details of the way people conduct them-lves, as the anecdotes he tells reveal. While making a Western, *Run r Cover* (1955, with James Cagney), he wanted to get away from the standard Indian scenes. 'What do they do,' he says, 'when they're *n* being Indians?' He devised a game, a sort of polo played with a h instead of a ball; but the episode, characteristically, was cut befo the film reached the public. Of Cagney, intriguingly, he said that l tried 'to bring out a kind of serenity in his personality'. Among tl actors he has directed, he cited James Dean as one of the mo stimulating to work with.

With Dean he was able freely to improvise, something he regards : an essential element in his style. He quoted the quarrel scene in *Reb Without a Cause*, when the boy comes home after the chicken run. Tl sequence was causing trouble, and Ray one evening asked James Dea to come to his house and work on it there. He himself would play tl father; and he stationed himself before a television set, switched to blank screen, so that he could watch Dean unobtrusively as he roam around, snatched up a bottle of milk from the refrigerator, thoug himself slowly into the situation. When the scene was right, in Dean and the director's understanding of it, he got the set designer to com over to his house so that the living-room set could be replanned on tl lines of his own room. The point, essentially, was the working out of mood in terms of a particular setting.

Twenty-five per cent of his work is probably as much as the avera film-maker (certainly the average Hollywood film-maker) expects be able wholly to endorse. Ray now has as much independence as mo directors. But he's had in the past the usual experiences of maki films not from choice but necessity, to work out a contract or get friend 'off the hook'. His second film, *A Woman's Secret* (1948, fro a Vicki Baum novel), was made, he implies, because Dore Scha caught him when his resistance was low and his spirits high after holiday. He expected little from this, or from *Flying Leathernec* (1951, John Wayne as a tough air-force pilot) or *Born To Be Bad* (195 Joan Fontaine as a tough girl on the make). He talks, as not : directors are ready to do, of the strain of gearing yourself up to a day work on a project you suspect from the start to be hopelessly wron

In other cases, the project had its possibilities, or the dissatisfactio came at a later stage. *Johnny Guitar* (1954), in which Joan Crawfo plays Vienna, the saloon owner who sits at her grand piano, dazzli in a white evening dress, while she waits for the lynching party, amus him in recollection. It was 'baroque – very baroque'. If you're filmi anything as bizarre as this story, of rivalry between Crawford a Mercedes McCambridge (her performance as leader of the posse, l admiringly says, was 'straight sulphuric acid'), then there's no point going less than all out. Much more seriously, Ray regards both *Bitt*

an Crawford in *Johnny Guitar*

ictory (1957, Curt Jurgens and Richard Burton in the desert war) ıd *The Savage Innocents* (1960) as flawed films; ambitious under-.kings whose themes somehow became muffled in the making.

The problems of *Savage Innocents* were the kind likely to crop up in)-productions, particularly when the subject is as tricky to cast as .is one. Ray did not want his Eskimos to be noble savages, conversing pidgin English. But somehow, as the film developed, his more fluent, .erary dialogue was sacrificed. He regrets, too, that the version seen ternationally had to be the one originally cut for the Italian market. he score had an Italian flavour; the jokes were a bit broader than .ey need be, to meet the Italian sense of humour; there was rather ore emphasis on blood and slaughter in the cutting. He wasn't tempting a second *Nanook*, which wasn't in any case practicable, but film which would make a particular moral point. The Eskimo and .e mountie, he says, have established a human contact; but this, when comes to the test, is not enough. The gap between cultures and vilizations cannot be jumped by good will alone.

This, at least, was the intention; and Ray feels the film blurs it, that .ere's a failure in clarity. Back one comes, in fact, to clarity, and his concern with it. One particular project, which Nicholas Ray fir mentioned to me four years ago and which remains unfilmed, seen to sum up a lot about him. It was to be a story called *Passport*, abou an American whose passport is stolen, and who finds that the loss of piece of paper is also a loss of identity. Searching for it, he would com one day upon a thief: a child, sitting by the sea, tearing up the passpo pages and throwing them into the water. The child's questio 'Where does the tide become national?' It's the sort of question, o feels, which Ray feels a need to keep asking, in however mar different forms he puts it.

Joseph Losey

Conversation with Joseph Losey is restless, stimulating, abrupt. W lead him off the track, he leads us off; one anecdote sparks anothe unrelated and probably off the record; he counters a question wi another question; he twists in his chair as he develops a point, the relaxes and smiles widely. Deeply concerned about problems communication, he has no difficulty in establishing an immediat personal contact with the people he's talking to. On the screen, o imagines, he finds communication as such not much more difficu though he repeatedly stresses its fundamental importance. Talking Resnais's *L'Année Dernière à Marienbad*, which he has recently see he emphasizes its technical mastery but is convinced that it will be a but incomprehensible to most audiences. And he clearly finds it little shocking that a film-maker should spend this kind of money c anything so indulgent. At the same time, he asserts, audiences a probably rather ahead of distributors in their appreciation and unde standing. This need to get a point across to an audience is a recurri theme. Of *The Criminal*, he says that his primary purpose was to bri home something about prison conditions to the general public; a he measures the film's success partly in these terms.

More has been written about *The Criminal* than about any oth film he has made; and most of the comments he regards as real perceptive come from France – this not only because the film had t bad luck in England to clash with *Saturday Night and Sunday Mornin* but because of the level of critical consideration. Losey was a friend the late Richard Winnington, whom he still regards as unequall among daily press critics. 'He just had this feeling for films.' He al respects Paul Dehn's enthusiasm. Shared with Ray, however, a doubts about just how much critics really know and care; and i enthusiasm he also misses at some levels of the industry in Britain.

In Hollywood, he says, 'relations between director and executi can be strained and full of misunderstandings, but even the most commercial people really do care about pictures. Over here, I sometimes get the impression that they just don't like films.' He's quick to qualify this with unstinting praise for British lighting cameramen ('you have some of the best in the world') and operators, for producers such as Anthony Havelock-Allan, for individual technicians and executives. But he cites an assistant director's comment – 'why kill yourself, it's only a film?' – which is clearly incomprehensible to a man whose involvement in his own work is total. 'I direct everything in the films I make,' he says, 'including second units.' On another level, he tells an anecdote of a British production executive who would not be convinced that audience tastes were moving in the direction of downbeat films. Losey quoted *Room at the Top* as an example, to be greeted with a surprised, 'But *Room at the Top* has a *happy* ending.'

Losey's own films, both here and in America, have mainly been made for independent producers. In America he worked very fast on *M* (twenty days), *The Prowler* (seventeen days) and *The Dividing Line* (twenty-three days). This, of course, was nothing out of the way by Hollywood standards and was possible because of the amount of pre-planning and rehearsal. In Britain it's more difficult to find rehearsal time and our studios are not geared to such rapid operation. In the case of *The Criminal*, for instance, he had to leave three scenes unshot because they couldn't be fitted into the schedule. In particular, a key one was to have established the character played by Jill Bennett as a drug addict, an omission which makes her first appearance in the film as it stands unintentionally bizarre.

In whatever country he's worked, Losey, like many directors, has hardly yet been in a position to film entirely on his own terms, initiating a project from scratch and developing it exactly as he wants. 'A director doesn't choose his subjects,' he says, 'they're offered to him.' But this is said without bitterness: it is one of the facts of a film-maker's life. He has planned productions which have never reached the screen – Brecht's *Galileo*, Strindberg's *The Father*, with Wilfrid Lawson, whom he directed on the stage in *The Wooden Dish* and regards as one of our great actors. *The Wild One* and *The Four Poster* were both films he might have made had he stayed in Hollywood.

Looking back to the Hollywood years, Losey names *The Prowler*, with its integration of decor and camera style into the narrative, as his favourite film from this period. He likes to co-operate with a production designer, someone whose function goes considerably beyond that usually taken by the art director; and, just as he has worked here with Richard Macdonald, a man who combines the unusual triple career

The Prowler: Evelyn Keyes, Van Heflin

of painter, advertising agency art director and (on Losey's Britis films) production designer, so on *The Prowler* his collaborator wa John Hubley. *The Prowler* is a film about pressure on character, th pressure of a violent action; and so, in a different sense, is *M*. 'I don' think of this as a remake of Lang's film, though I did use a couple o his ideas. I wanted the man to be more sympathetic, for one thing The main trouble was the establishing of this kind of subject in a American setting – I couldn't believe myself in the idea of the whol underworld ganging up against the killer.' The film was so heavily cu in this country that we have never had a chance to see it as he intended

He is not entirely satisfied now with *The Dividing Line*, on whic there were casting problems, or *The Boy with Green Hair*, which h regards as a bit too sentimental. He accepts, tentatively, a criticis that it's the liberal characters and the way their attitudes are expresse which now date *The Dividing Line*, while its feeling for latent violenc remains as strong as ever.

On these films Losey was working within the socially critical frame work of the post-war American cinema, in a tradition allowing for kind of mental toughness that has never been part of British film ɿaking. On the whole, we protect our institutions. 'You have the most uccessful class system in the world,' he comments. Coming to terms vith British life, to the point where he felt he could give it valid xpression on the screen, would be a problem for any director of this emperament; and in Losey's case it must have been accentuated by he hole-and-corner conditions in which he had to work during his rst years here. But he has never, he affirms, taken on a project he hought had nothing to offer him, and prefers television commercials o unrewarding feature work – 'Though I have turned down one or wo commercials as well.' The efforts to re-establish himself, the reach with Hollywood, must have been accompanied by deep rustrations, though any scars are kept well hidden. Return to Hollywood is not impossible: but Losey has never been prepared to pay the rice of turning informer.

To date, Losey regards *The Criminal* as by far the most successful of is British Films. From *The Sleeping Tiger*, in which psychiatrist lexander Knox became hazardously involved with Dirk Bogarde as psychotic adolescent, he looks back with affection only to two of the ove scenes between Bogarde and Alexis Smith. *The Gypsy and the Gentleman*, his solitary period film, was elaborately designed to give he effect of a series of Rowlandson prints. He took on this fanciful egency novelette, with its wild gipsy heroine (Melina Mercouri) and ory of a stolen inheritance, largely for what he thought could be done ith it visually. But the film was overlaid with a sentimental score, ancelling out the much more robust visual style. *Blind Date*, again, as not a subject he would necessarily have chosen; and was in fact aken on after another and more attractive project had fallen through. problem here was to get over the initial improbability of the plot, hich all hinges on the fact that a man who discovers a corpse doesn't eally look at it properly. To counteract this, Losey worked for aximum credibility in the characters and, again with Richard Macdonald, in the settings of police station and artist's studio.

Losey's picture of the police in *Blind Date* met strong opposition, nd his view of prison life in *The Criminal* has been similarly challenged. But everything I showed in the film has since been reported in the ress,' he insists. It was the prison scenes that really concerned him, nd again he found himself accepting a subject because he was tracted by some aspects rather than by the whole. He took advice om someone he would identify only as 'the head of the underworld London' as well as from prison officials, and the film reflects the life professional crime as he encountered it. We raised the question of s attitude to brutality, the apparent fascination with the facts and

Eva: Jeanne Moreau

face of violence. 'People who say I'm fascinated by violence ar fascinated by it themselves,' was the crisp retort. Someone, wit Buñuel in mind, suggested that there was no real reason why an artis shouldn't build his work around an obsessive violence, and Lose pounced on the point. 'De Sade, after all, produced a great deal tha was psychologically and socially valuable.' For his own part, howeve 'I hate violence. I don't consider that I exploit it on the screen. Bu I'll tell you of a director who does. . . .' And he named an eminer American film-maker usually thought to be above such considera tions. The standard criticism of his work, Losey says, is not that h enjoys violence but that he encourages overacting. 'I am interested i larger-than-life characters, not overacted ones. I like to work wit actors like Patrick Magee who have a really creative contribution t make.'

He should be doing this on his next picture, which stars the explosiv combination of Jeanne Moreau and Stanley Baker. The film is *Ev* adapted from a James Hadley Chase story about a hack writer and high-priced call-girl; the producers are French, and the picture is t be shot in Italy. After this, there are plans for *Holiday*, to be filmed i

Greece for Carl Foreman's company, a possible collaboration with Marguerite Duras, and a version, if the production can be set up, of Alun Owen's *No Trams to Lime Street*.

The first requirement Losey makes of a film-maker is that he should have a 'signature', an immediately recognizable style. His off-the-cuff list of British directors who have, have had, or could have it: Carol Reed, Alexander Mackendrick, Lindsay Anderson, Seth Holt, John Guillermin. *Saturday Night and Sunday Morning*, for all its qualities, misses out on this point, as does *Room at the Top* ('Clayton's signature here is Signoret'). He finds the indispensable signature in *L'Avventura*, which he greatly admires, and, with reservations, in *Breathless* ('But ren't they more kids playing at film-making than kids in the film playing at life?') There's a craftsman's impatience with some of the *ouvelle vague* 'innovations' which, he says, are only old tricks efurbished.

His own craftsmanship is not in doubt, however violently critics disagree about the uses to which it's put. A glance through the British nd French press comments on *The Criminal* makes instructive reading. 'Losey's thought has never been more lucid, nor its expression more rigorous'; this is 'a style of admirable elegance, and a hard, iolent, passionate style'; he creates 'a pitiless world, into which only intelligence throws a sharp, dazzling, necessary light'. 'A phoney film t may be, but it is one for the students'; it is 'all done in saw-mill style, high-pitched buzz interrupted by shrieks'; it 'never properly stablishes its own level of shock and conscience'. The nationalities proclaim themselves, though if anyone should be in doubt the second three quotations are British. Are these irreconcilable differences? Losey, one feels, would like to prove they are not; and the greater freedom in choice of subjects that he's now acquiring may give him the pportunity.

Nicholas Ray: films as director

948: *They Live by Night*
949: *A Woman's Secret, Knock on Any Door*
950: *In a Lonely Place, Born to be Bad*
951: *On Dangerous Ground, Flying Leathernecks*
952: *The Lusty Men*
954: *Johnny Guitar*
955: *Run for Cover, Rebel Without a Cause*
956: *Hot Blood, Bigger Than Life*
957: *The True Story of Jesse James (The James Brothers)*

1958: *Bitter Victory, Wind Across the Everglades, Party Girl*
1960: *The Savage Innocents*
1961: *King of Kings*
1962: *55 Days at Peking*
1968: *Wha–at*

Joseph Losey: films as director

1939: *Pete Roleum and his Cousins* (short)
1941: *A Child Went Forth, Youth Gets a Break* (shorts)
1945: *A Gun in His Hand* (short)
1948: *The Boy with Green Hair*
1949: *The Lawless (The Dividing Line)*
1951: *The Prowler, M, The Big Night*
1952: *Stranger on the Prowl (Encounter)*
1954: *The Sleeping Tiger* (under name of Victor Hanbury)
1955: *A Man on the Beach*
1956: *The Intimate Stranger* (under name of Joseph Walton)
1957: *Time Without Pity, The Gypsy and the Gentleman*
1959: *Blind Date*
1960: *The Criminal, First on the Road* (short)
1962: *The Damned, Eve*
1963: *The Servant*
1964: *King and Country*
1966: *Modesty Blaise*
1967: *Accident*
1968: *Boom, The Secret Ceremony*
1970: *Figures in a Landscape*
1971: *The Go-Between*

Abraham Polonsky
n correspondence with William
Pechter, 1962

n 1949 a writer, whose experience, with the exception of two previous creenplays and two unmemorable novels, had been primarily in radio, nade an adaptation of an unsuccessful journalistic novel to the screen, nd directed a film of it. The event would not seem to be a particularly uspicious one nor much of a novelty for Hollywood, where every other ay finds one hack adapting the work of another hack. Nor would it have een much more promising to know that the film made use of several lements that were sufficiently familiar – the bad-good guy involved in he rackets who finally goes straight, the ingénue *who tries to reform im, etc. Yet, apparently, to have known all this was not to know enough. How else to account for the fact that out of it all was created an original, noving, and even beautiful work whose only tangency with clichés was at he point at which it transformed and transcended them? I think it is ccounted for by that phenomenon which never ceases to be somehow oth inexplicable and unpredictable: the presence of an artist.*

But the event was, perhaps, not quite so unpredictable as I may, omewhat Hollywoodishly, have made it sound. The artist's name was braham Polonsky, and his film was Force of Evil*; previously, he had* *written the original scenario for the film* Body and Soul. Body and Sou *did not lack acclaim; although independently produced, it won a Academy Award, and was financially successful.* Force of Evil *wa without acclaim or appreciation; noticed only by the British fil periodicals, it was allowed to die its quiet death, a gangster film with onl muted violence, a love story without romantic apotheosis, a Hollywoo film without the Happy Ending. Both* Sight and Sound *and* Sequenc *had cited it as among the most original films of its year, and it sti occasionally crops up in catalogues of neglected works. Lindsa Anderson, in his close analysis of the last sequence of* On the Waterfron *which appeared in* Sight and Sound *several years ago, invoked* Forc of Evil *as foil to that film's operatic dishonesty. The habitual Britis reader may have caught the aptness of the comparison; for the America one, it must have been merely a little baffling.*

In theme and meaning, Body and Soul *and* Force of Evil *form a extraordinary unity. In each, the hero, played in both cases with combination of tough cynicism and urban dreaminess by the late Joh Garfield at his most characteristic, allows himself to become involve with certain forces of corruption, only, finally, to revolt against the and attempt to wrench himself free. In both films, the hero is not move to this final breach without first having caused some irrevocable violenc to those most close to him, and both films end not with some cheap an easy redemption, but deep in* Angst *and ambiguity. 'What can you do Kill me? Everybody dies,' are the final words of* Body and Soul, *as th fighter says them to the gambler whose fight he has refused to throw. Th effect is not entirely pessimistic; there is a certain heroic implication the fighter's assertion of his moral triumph, inalterable even in death still, the fact remains that a life is not this casually disposed of, and th audience demands some compensation for the lack of final Uplift. Th it got, in* Body and Soul, *in the physical excitement of the prizefight scenes, photographed so dynamically by James Wong Howe on (roller skates, and in the reliable familiarity of the fundamental stor line: ambitious slum boy battles way up to success. It is the kind of stor that allows the audience the illicit thrill of a vicarious participation in th somewhat unscrupulous rise of the hero without the guilt that belong properly to him. So, despite the frequently rich and even lyrical languag of the film, its often striking images of city life, and the sense of flexib and sensitive human relationships which managed to cluster about th success story's rigid central structure, despite, that is to say, th presence of artistry, it was officially recognized by the Academy Motion Picture Art and Sciences as a work of art.*

Force of Evil *is not so immediately likeable a film; it is without suc* direct compensations for its underlying sadness. Unlike the fighter of Body and Soul, Joe Morse, the hero of Force of Evil, is not so simply and understandably the product of social determinations. We first see him as a successful lawyer; he is not fighting to escape poverty, but to annex greater wealth. Nor is he unaware of the nature of his involvement, or without moral understanding. One is never certain that the fighter of Body and Soul is wholly aware of his moral predicament; but Joe Morse acknowledges full responsibility, without even pleading the excuse of weakness. By his own admission, he is 'strong enough to get a part of the corruption, but not strong enough to resist it'. But this is not so much weakness as a perversion of strength, a defect not in quality but in kind. The progress of Force of Evil is that of the painfully gradual burgeoning of a moral imagination – if you prefer, a conscience. It is not miraculously achieved by romantic love, but only attained after the death of Joe's older brother, whom he had tried both to advance and to protect within the racket in which they become involved. It is the relationship of the two brothers which is the central love story of the film – the Freudian 'family romance' – a love thwarted mutually by guilt, and ending in anguish. In terms of plot, the film ends utterly without stereotypic satisfactions: the older brother is killed; Joe is about to confess to the police, and inevitably to be punished; there is no final, solipsistic kiss. 'I decided to help,' are Joe's last words as the film concludes, after he has found his dead brother's battered body. It is a moment entirely free from the pieties which customarily attend such a regeneration, nor has it any of that sense of straining to engage some good, grey abstraction like 'Society', which hangs so heavily over the last sequence of On the Waterfront. Force of Evil ends in moral awakening, but it reaches out not so much towards society as towards community, even communion; a sense of the oneness of human involvement without any diminution of that involvement's ineluctable guilt.

Were this all, one might have simply a film of the tenderness, sensitivity, and, I believe, somewhat vitiating softness of, say, They Live by Night. Even Sight and Sound tended to relegate Force of Evil to the status of a sympathetic but 'minor' film; I think this is other than the case. The film was said to be overly literary, and there is no doubt that it is a work which relies heavily on its language; perhaps, we are still not entirely free of the tyrannical dogma that language is not properly an element of film. To observe that the language of Force of Evil is beautiful in itself may not be quite to the point. The impression of that language is of for the first time really hearing, on the screen, the sound of city speech, with its special repetitions and elisions, cadence and inflection, inarticulateness and crypto-poetry; much as Odets had brought it to the stage. As in

Odets, the effect is naturalistic, and, as in Odets, it is achieved by an extreme degree of mannerism, artifice, and stylization. But the astonishing thing about Force of Evil, more obvious now, perhaps, in the light o such more overtly experimental works as Hiroshima, Mon Amour, i the way in which the image works with the word. Nothing is duplicated or supererogatory. Even in so simple an instance as that of the heroine' face in close-up, as the first person narrative runs 'Doris wanted me t make love to her', is the relationship of word to image complementar rather than redundant. The sound-track is the image slantwise; refracte through an individual consciousness, and, to that extent, interpreted Throughout the film, Joe is constantly commenting upon the action telling us not only what he and the others think, but even describing hi own, overt actions as we see him engaging in them. It is this kind o awareness and volition which is alien to the conventional melodramati hero; and it is interesting to note that it is a departure from the nove which is related in flatly omniscient third person. The effect of all thi off-repetition, with its language overlapping image and language over lapping language, is finally quite different from that of the very simila devices of Hiroshima, Mon Amour. In that film, the final effect is merel rhetorical and consciously artistic; in Force of Evil, the language take on the quality of incantation, and imparts an almost choric resonance t the Cain and Abel myth which lies at the film's centre.

The more one sees Force of Evil, the closer one gets to the film centre, the more one becomes aware of that central myth, and the forma means by which it is exposed. The language becomes a kind of insisten music, and the images move congruently with an extraordinary purit and freedom. A brief conversation is composed from a remote angl above a gracefully curving stairway; the moment exists both in an independent of the plot; and, independently, it is startlingly beautifu Such imagery proliferates throughout the film, from the simplest of con versational exchanges to the complexly moving vision of Joe runnin senselessly down a deserted Wall Street at night, knowing that neve again will he be able to return to his 'fine office up in the clouds'. Force c Evil is, actually, a very impure film; it is literary and dramatic, but onl insofar as the film is a literary and dramatic medium, and no furthe Beneath and beyond that, there is the autonomous beauty of poet diction; the aesthetic paradox that what is harrowing in life may be the and be also beautiful in art. And the final passage of the film, in which, i the pervasive greyness of the early morning, Joe discovers his brother body at the base of an arching bridge, from the desolate rocks upo which it has been discarded, 'like an old rag', is both immensely harrow ing and starkly beautiful. It is a descent to 'the bottom of the world', to *kind of hell; the symbolic death that must be suffered before regeneration. 'Because, if a man can live so long, and have his whole life come out like rubbish, then something was horribly wrong . . . and I decided to help.'*

[*The 'interview' with Abraham Polonsky related below was conducted entirely through correspondence. I have taken the liberty of some slight rearrangement so that there might be a clear relation of answer to question, but the words remain unchanged. Therefore, while the exchanges may occasionally approximate the give and take of conversation, they may be accepted as having the value of written reflection, such as that may be.*] – William Pechter

PECHTER: *Would you begin by giving me some idea of your background before you began working in films? Somewhere I picked up the information that you originally wrote for radio, and, if my memory doesn't play tricks, I recall reading a radio script of yours in the old* Quarterly of Film, Radio, and Television. *I also seem to remember hearing that you taught for a while at the University of Southern California and even the City College of New York, although I am not sure of the chronology (i.e., before or after film-making), and virtually certain that I must have dreamed the latter. Would you also refer to your published fiction and film criticism?*

POLONSKY: I led the usual restless street life: gang (East Side); schoolboy (P.S. 32, 57, De Witt Clinton); teacher (CCNY, A.B.); Law (Columbia); volunteer in politics (Democrat, Anarchist, Radical, Confused). I taught at City College from 1932 to the war; never taught at the University of Southern California. I am familiar with the learned professions (teaching and law), the vagrant ones (sea, farm, factory), and the eternal ones (marriage, fatherhood, art, science). The most extraordinary shock in my life was not the war which I survived, but the films which I did not. I always wrote, produced little motion in life and never stopped talking.

My first novel (*The Discoverers*) was accepted, announced, advertised by Modern Age Books and then withdrawn as unreadable. I retired to silence in art, action in politics, and gibberish in radio (Columbia Workshop, Orson Welles, Goldbergs, and I forget). Two potboilers (Simon and Schuster, Little, Brown). The war (O.S.S.). My blueberry pie was Paramount.

Excluding the movies for the moment, I managed a semi-serious return to the novel with *The World Above*, and, after being blacklisted, *The Season of Fear*. These attempts were laced with some short stories, criticism, and genteel scholarly editing (*Hollywood Quarterly, Contemporary Reader*).

The guerrilla life I pretended to practise in the war I played with some amusement and frequent disgust in the jungle of TV as a blacklisted writer. Likewise in films. Those minor victories and major defeats admit no obituaries at the moment.

How did you begin your work in films?

By accident. I signed with Paramount before going overseas. However appalled as I was by the industry and its product, the medium overwhelmed me with a language I had been trying to speak all my life.

Since I am under the impression that it is not extensive, would you mention all of your screen credits, official and unofficial, if the latter case is such?

Credits. *Golden Earrings:* direction, Mitchell Leisen. Assigned to an incredible romantic melodramatic stew, I painstakingly studied gipsy life under the Nazis (they were incinerated) and very cleverly worked the whole thing around to something else. The film, starring Marlene Dietrich, appeared as an incredible romantic melodramatic stew. I never could sit through it. I know there isn't a single word or scene of mine in it, but I was instructed to rejoice in the credit which I shared with two old hands, Helen Deutsch and Frank Butler.

Body and Soul: original screenplay; direction, Robert Rossen.

Force of Evil: screenplay with Ira Wolfert from his novel, *Tucker's People*; my direction.

I Can Get It for You Wholesale: screenplay based on Weidman's own treatment which simply kept the title of the novel. A comedy of sorts, directed by Mike Gordon with Dan Dailey, Susan Hayward. It was a stopgap for me to return to Europe to write another book and set up *Mario and the Magician.* Before I left, Thomas Mann told me he felt his exile was beginning all over again since fascism was inevitable in America. The novel I completed years later. No one wanted to finance the film.

I returned to Hollywood and made a deal with Sol Siegel at Twentieth to write and direct a picture, but the blacklist intervened.

Was your scenario for Body and Soul *a wholly original work, or was it derived from some other source?*

It's an original screenplay. A folk tale from the Empire city.

Was Rossen to direct the movie from the time of the script's inception or did he only come to do it through the contingencies of film production?

Rossen was hired after the script was done.

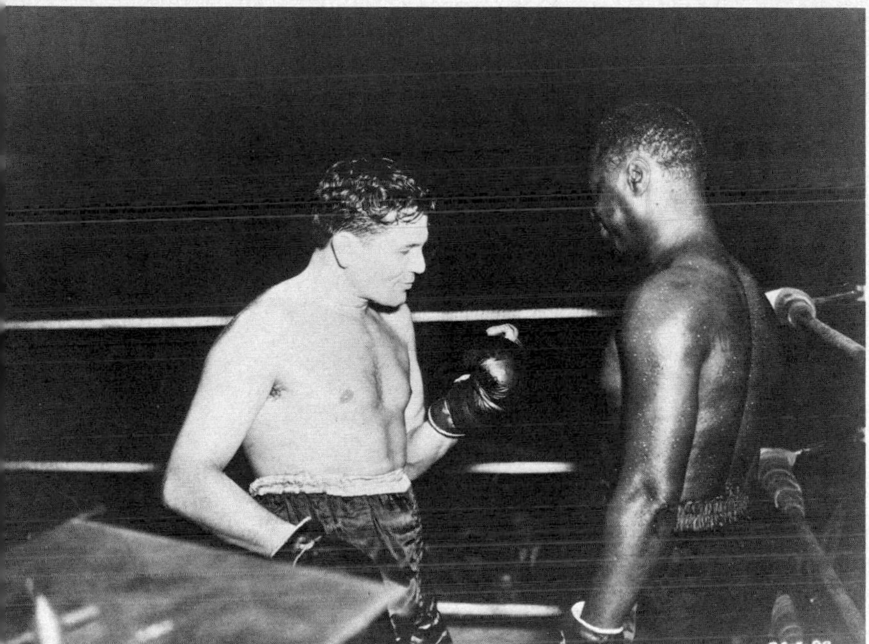

Body and Soul: John Garfield, Canada Lee

Did your work on Body and Soul *end with the scenario?*

No.

Were you present on the set during shooting?

Continuously.

Of course, it is easy to look knowing in retrospect, but to judge from Rossen's other work, Body and Soul *would seem to have closer affinities with* Force of Evil *than with the other films of his, even in the elusive matter of visual style. Or am I just second guessing?*

There was a struggle during the shooting to prevent Rossen from rewriting the script and changing the ending. In fact he shot an alternate finish in which the fighter is killed and ends up with his head in a garbage can. I think a comparison of *Body and Soul* with *The Hustler* might indicate not only the uses Rossen made of the former but where his temperament and style inevitably lead him.

Are you satisfied with the realization of Body and Soul *as a film?*

I liked *Body and Soul*. It was a surprise to see something I had written become film. I have an animal faith that survives moral weakness and defeat. To urge this against Rossen's metaphysical identity with every-day cynicism and the journalism of sense and sex indicated the realities of film-making. Our resources on the set were immense: Garfield James Wong Howe, Robert Aldrich, Lyons and Parrish, Don Weis. Pevney. A slew of directors emerged from the film. Rossen's talent is force applied everywhere without let-up. My only concern was to save it from parody, except where deliberately I had kidded *Golden Boy* and that dear old violin. However, I'm not so sure any more that the obvious isn't one of the strengths of film language. If so it violates a bias of my nature.

What attracted you about Tucker's People *as an original source?*

Experiment. Garfield and Robert suggested that I direct. I had already been brooding over this notion. Being a novice didn't prevent me from sharing all the illusions and frustrations of more seasoned writers. I was under fire long before I knew I had volunteered.

I knew *Tucker's People*. It had an allegory, true then and even more bitterly apt today; a milieu and characters familiar as my own habits a hint of the language of the unconscious I could use as dialogue. In realization, necessities of the medium evaporated the allegory, leaving great uncharted reefs of symbolism to wreck the audience; the people emerged except where I agreed to wrong casting; and the language almost obeyed my intention to play an equal role with the actor and visual image and not run along as illustration, information, and mere verbal gesture (wisecracks, conventional middle-class slang, elevated notions drawn from the armoury of Longfellow and Hemingway).

In the course of adaptation, you altered the novel rather radically excising some characters and events, combining and condensing others What particular problems did you feel were fundamental to your decisions in making the adaptation? I don't mean so much with regard to Tucker's People *in particular as with the question of adapting to the screen in general.*

I no longer remember anything except the days Wolfert and I spent endlessly talking along the beaches. Under the windy sun we didn't reason so much as proclaim discoveries. In effect, we eliminated the discursive power of the book and substituted for it so to speak centres of suggestion. We re-imagined the novel as if it were an aborigine again. Then it became obvious that some characters would play larger roles and others disappear. Adapting a book to film is fundamentally a moral crisis. Assuming the intention is serious, the book is not chosen to be translated for non-readers but because still embedded in the conception is a whole unrealized life whose language is a motion of images. Where a book is unfulfilled a frightful problem arises. The film, if successful, is a critique of the author's failures. I am a coward here and prefer my own stories.

Do you have any particular conception of the nature of the medium? One of the original reviewers of Force of Evil *(Robert Hatch in* The Nation, *as I recall) suspected the presence of blank verse, and was duly horrified; but even admirers of the film have characterized it as 'literary'. Does this have any meaning to you? Do you have any ideas about the relation of word to image in the film; yours, and, perhaps, the film in general?*

I've heard them talk in talking pictures. Might talkies be like the opera? The main thing is the music but O the joy when the singers act and the songs are poetry. Let's pretend, I assumed for *Tucker's People* (*Force of Evil*) that the three elements, visual image, actor, word, are equals. (After all, the human personality is the medium of total human expressiveness. After all, language has been a medium for an art or two.) I didn't project anything important, just an experiment in which each of my resources was freed of the dominance of the other two. I was too inexperienced to invent novel visual images or evoke great performances. And certainly there was nothing in my literary record to suggest a New Voice. All I tried to do was use the succession of visual images, the appearances of human personality in the actors, and the rhythm of words in unison or counterpoint. I varied the speed, intensity, congruence and conflict for design, emotion and goal, sometimes separating the three elements, sometimes using two or three together. As for the language, I merely freed it of the burden of literary psychology and the role of crutch to the visual image. Blank verse? No. But the babble of the unconscious, yes, as much as I could, granted the premise that I was committed to a representational film. It was a method I would have tried again and again until solved. After all, we had that big Hollywood machine which the success of *Body and Soul* had delivered into our hands and we didn't mind seeing what we could do with all that horsepower. But the blacklist took the machine away from us. While we had possession, like those bicycle fanatics at Kitty Hawk, we couldn't wait to waken in the morning, knowing that each day would surprise us. We had the right feelings. Only our plane never flew.

Would you say you have been influenced by any other film-makers?

Vigo.

Body and Soul

Mention has been made in a way I think might be valid of Odets as a literary influence. What is your opinion of this?

We both derive from Jewish jokes and street quarrels. I live dangled between the formal and argot without solution. I've tried to avoid American Standard Movie dialogue which is a genuine Hollywood convention. But I can write it and have for a living.

What film-makers do you particularly admire?

I like going to the movies.

What Hollywood films have you thought commendable since the late 40s?

I seem to remember liking some but I can't remember which.

Is there an identity of theme and meaning between Body and Soul *and* Force of Evil*?*

Yes, but in *Force of Evil* every character and situation is compromised by reality while *Body and Soul* is a folk tale.

Eric Bentley has made the point that in both Elia Kazan's On the Waterfront *and Arthur Miller's* A View from the Bridge *there is*

Force of Evil: John Garfield

scarcely beneath the surface, an apologetic for each of their respective positions on political informing, a certain acting out of private crises; informing being the crucial act in both works, good in the former and evil in the latter. Force of Evil *ends with the hero about to confess to the police, and 'help' them. I do not mean to suggest that the final act is ever simply this, but do you feel that there is any political parable underlying the conclusion to your film?*

Not a parable, a fact. The hero is about to confess to the police because that was the way we could get a seal. There was an allegory underlying the film. It got lost somewhere and had nothing to do with confession or avoidance. Bentley is certainly right in his estimate of those works although the distinction between good informing and bad escapes me. One informs not only to escape punishment and regain acceptance but to share once again in the authority of the state. It is a hard life outside the pale.

Do you believe or know that you were blacklisted?

I know it and I believe it.

How did you discover this?

I was told by the studio, my agent, the newspapers, Congress, and my landlord.

How is one blacklisted; I mean, what is the typical nature of the process?

One is named in a hearing by an informer, or one is summoned to the hearing in person. The consequences are the same.

Do you know of particular individuals who were behind the blacklist, or was its authority always kept anonymous?

The cold war was behind the blacklist and everyone participated, from those on the political right through those who had no politics. It was like collaboration under the Nazis. And it was like the resistance. The spectrum took in everything human including the inhuman.

Did you ever appear before the House Un-American Activities Committee?

Yes.

Was there any opportunity for compromise in order to 'clear' yourself?

Then and now and frequently in between.

John Cogley, in his Report on Blacklisting, *observes that there was virtually no political content in the films of the blacklisted, and when it did exist it was usually in the form of so generalized a commitment to democratic ideals and justifiable revolution as could be subscribed to by any member of the audience but the most avid Hitlerite. Do you agree? Would you ascribe this to lack of intent, or lack of accomplishment? Or lack of talent?*

Hollywood radicals were mainly moral humanists and their films when they reflected anything at all showed a concern for the suppressed elements in human life. Political programming of any sort, left, middle, right, couldn't ever appear because producers wanted to make money. When political programming did appear as in the so-called anti-communist pictures they were made in deference to the climate and not from the usual expectation of profits. Cogley's argument that blacklisting radicals is silly because they're too stupid or talentless to use the film for direct Marxist propaganda is jejune. He is talking about journalism, not story telling.

Do you have any thoughts on the career of Edward Dmytryk, who went from the Hollywood Ten to 'exoneration', and eventually was to film such a tribute to conformity as The Caine Mutiny*?*

He probably thought it was capitalist realism.

It has been suggested that John Garfield's political difficulties and debarment from Hollywood work were a considerable influence in accelerating his early death. Do you have any opinion on this?

Yes. He defended his streetboy's honour and they killed him for it.

In the publisher's blurb for The Season of Fear, *it was implied that you left film-making voluntarily in order 'to go abroad and devote yourself] to serious fiction'. Aside from the thinly veiled, characteristic cultural snobbery, is there any truth in this?*

No.

Inasmuch as you have any self-image, do you regard yourself primarily as a novelist or film-maker? Or both?

Neither. If I were younger you might say I had promise.

Were you aware of the sympathetic reception accorded Force of Evil *in* Sight and Sound *and* Sequence*?*

Yes.

Was their appreciation of any personal importance to you?

Pure oxygen.

Was Body and Soul *a financial success?*

Very much so.

Was Force of Evil *commercially successful?*

No.

Do you have any criticisms of the latter film's distribution?

It got lost in the general dissolution of Enterprise studios. Had we stayed in business we could have rescued it and made some money.

How did you come to use Beatrice Pearson?

She was brought to my attention by Martin Jurow, now a considerable producer himself. He worked for our company at that time.

Where had you seen her previously?

Nowhere.

What became of her?

She was in a few films and disappeared. They didn't know how to use her.

In what work are you engaged at present?

Grub Street.

Have you had any opportunity to make films since Force of Evil*?*

No.

Have you imagined any new subjects you would have particularly liked to work into a film?

Indeed I have.

Do you see any possibility for your prospective return to work in the film?

No.

What are your plans for the future?

None.

The interviewing of an artist is chancy; the pitfalls are familiar. On one hand, there is the kind of gulling Lindsay Anderson suffered at the hands of John Ford in his well-known Sequence *interview; on the other, those dreary chronologies of how The Studio mutilated this film, and how They butchered that. Both alternatives may be valuable in their way (and the Anderson piece, I believe, does reveal, even inadvertently, a good deal of Ford's nature as an artist), but I was interested in achieving neither. Existing somewhere in that uncharted area between the put-on and the death toll, I tend immodestly to think that my 'encounter' with Abraham Polonsky was something of a success. In anticipating critical intelligence of the artist, one proceeds at one's own risk. In Polonsky, I found this sort of intelligence, and the ability to articulate it.*

Not all of the questions were answered as thoroughly as they might have been, but I conceived my role not as inquisitor; I was not out to 'get all the facts'; rather, to open up certain areas for discussion, to that extent which Polonsky was interested in going into them. Politically, for example, it may be observed that, although the spectres of the blacklist and the House Un-American Activities Committee are pointedly raised, no question is put as to Polonsky's actual political affiliations. I don't think of this as an evasion. My own attitude towards the pursuit of this line of questioning (from an anti-communist position, it may not be irrelevant to add) is simply: So what? The fact remains that Abraham Polonsky, having earned the right to work in Hollywood on the terms which Hollywood unfailingly understands, those of having proven the ability to show a profit, was denied the exercise of that less-than-glorious right. The fact is that since 1949 a film-maker whom I regard as one of the richest talents to have appeared in Hollywood in the past fifteen years (and, I believe, the richest literary talent to have appeared in the American film) has not been able to work in films. One need not respond emotionally to that fact. One need not respond emotionally to any fact.

Abraham Polonsky: films as director

1949: *Force of Evil*
1968: *Tell them Willie Boy is Here*

Orson Welles talking to Juan Cobos, Miguel Rubio and José Antonio Pruneda, 1965

That Welles, the ageing enfant terrible *of the American cinema, is still the youngest indisputably great American director is an ominous symptom of decadence in the industry as a whole. It can even be argued that Welles's films are now less American than European in outlook, and that in ten years or less, there may be no American cinema of great artistic significance. Even today, the best American films represent the creative spasms of the last gasp instead of the first breath. No matter. With* The Trial, *Welles's career has taken a curious turn. This Man from Mars who projected radio dynamics to that RKO-Radio classic,* Citizen Kane, *has gradually gone sour on the sound-track. The ear of the expatriate has lost contact with the nuances of American speech. It may be no accident that Welles has gradually turned away from the psychological density of the biography (*Citizen Kane*) and the filmed novel (*The Magnificent Ambersons*) to the psychological abstractions of fantasy (*Lady from Shanghai*), allegory (*Touch of Evil*), fable (*Mr Arkadin*) and hallucination (*The Trial*). The conventional American diagnosis of his career is decline, pure and simple, but decline is never pure and never simple. Welles began his career on such a high plateau that the most precipitous decline would not affect his place in the*

Pantheon. Citizen Kane *is still the work which influenced the cinema more profoundly than any American film since* Birth of a Nation. *If the 30s belonged to Lubitsch's subtle grace and unobtrusive cutting, the 40s belong to the Wellesian resurrection of Murnau's portentous camera angles. The decade of plots gave way to a decade of themes, and the American cinema had lost its innocence and charm forever. From the beginning, Welles imposed a European temperament on the American cinema. Even today, Arthur Penn acknowledges the influence of Welles. Certainly the cinema is no poorer for having been injected with a Wellesian intelligence.* – A. S.

COBOS: *In* The Trial, *it seems that you were making a severe criticism of the abuse of power; unless it concerns something more profound. Perkins appeared as a sort of Prometheus. . . .*

WELLES: He is also a little bureaucrat. I consider him guilty.

Why do you say he is guilty?

Who knows? He belongs to something that represents evil and that, at the same time, is part of him. He is not guilty as accused, but he is guilty all the same. He belongs to a guilty society, he collaborates with it. In any case, I am not a Kafka analyst.

A version of the scenario exists with a different ending. The executioners stab K to death.

That ending didn't please me. I believe that in that case it is a question of a 'ballet' written by a pre-Hitler Jewish intellectual. After the death of six million Jews, Kafka would not have written that. It seemed to me to be pre-Auschwitz. I don't want to say that my ending was good, but it was the only solution. I had to move into high gear, even if it was only for several instants.

One of the constants of your work is the struggle for liberty and the defence of the individual.

A struggle for dignity. I absolutely disagree with those words of art, those novels, those films that, these days, speak about despair. I do not think that an artist may take total despair as a subject: we are too close to it in daily life. This kind of subject can be used only when life is less dangerous and more clearly affirmative.

In the transposition of The Trial *to the cinema, there is a fundamental change; in Kafka's book, K's character is more passive than in the film.*

I do not believe that passive characters are appropriate to drama. I have nothing against Antonioni, for example, but, in order to interest ıe, the characters must do something, from a dramatic point of view, ou understand.

Was The Trial *an old project?*

I once said that a good film could be drawn from the novel, but I ıyself didn't think of doing it. A man came to see me and told me he elieved he could find money so that I could make a film in France. Ie gave me a list of films and asked that I choose. And from that list f fifteen films I chose the one that, I believe, was the best: *The Trial.* ince I couldn't do a film written by myself, I chose Kafka.

What films do you really want to do?

Mine. I have drawers full of scenarios I've written.

In The Trial, *was the long travelling shot of Katina Paxinou dragging he trunk while Anthony Perkins talks to her a tribute to Brecht?*

I did not see it that way. There was a long scene with her which ısted ten minutes and which, moreover, I cut on the eve of the Paris remière. I only saw the film as a whole once. We were still in the rocess of doing the mixing, and then the première fell on us. At the ıst moment I abridged the ten-minute scene. It should have been the est scene in the film and it wasn't. Something went wrong, I guess. I on't know why, but it didn't succeed. The subject of that scene was ee will. It was tinged with *comédie noire*; that was my hobby-horse. ıs you know, it is always directed against the machine and in favour f freedom.

When Joseph K sees the shadow-show at the end, with the story of the uard, the door, etc., does this relate to your own thoughts on the inema?

It concerns a technical problem posed by the story to be told. If it ere told at that precise moment, the public would go to sleep; that is hy I tell it at the beginning and only recall it at the end. The effect ıen is equivalent to telling the story at that moment and I was able in ıis way to tell it in a few seconds. But, in any case, I am not the judge.

A critic who admires your work very much said that, in The Trial, *you ere repeating yourself. . . .*

Exactly, I repeated myself. I believe we do it all the time. We always ake up certain elements again. How can it be avoided? An actor's oice always has the same timbre and, consequently, he repeats himself. t is the same for a singer, a painter. . . . There are always certain things at come back, for they are part of one's personality, of one's style. these things didn't come into play, a personality would be so complex t it would become impossible to identify it.

Anthony Perkins in *The Trial*

It is not my intention to repeat myself but in my work there shoul certainly be references to what I have done in the past. Say what yo will, but *The Trial* is the best film I have ever made. One repeats onesel only when one is tired. Well, I wasn't tired. I have never been as happ as when I made this film.

How did you shoot Anthony Perkins's long running scene?

We built a very long platform and the camera was placed on rolling chair.

But it's enormously fast!

Yes, but I had a Yugoslav runner to push my camera.

What is astonishing in your work is this continued effort to brin solutions to the problems posed by directing. . . .

The cinema is still very young and it would be completely ridiculou not to succeed in finding new things for it. If only I could make mor films! Do you know what happened with *The Trial*? Two weeks befor our departure from Paris for Yugoslavia, we were told that there w no possibility of having a single set built there because the produc ad already made another film in Yugoslavia and hadn't paid his ebts. That's why it was necessary to use that abandoned station. I had lanned a completely different film.

Everything had to be invented at the last minute because physically ny film had an entirely different conception. It was based on an bsence of sets. And this gigantism I have been reproached for is, in art, due to the fact that the only set I possessed was that old abandoned tation. An empty railroad station is immense! The production, as I ad sketched it, comprised sets that gradually disappeared. The umber of realistic elements were to become fewer and fewer and the ublic would become aware of it, to the point where the scene would e reduced to free space as if everything had dissolved.

The movement of the actors and the camera in relation to each other n your films is very beautiful.

That is a visual obsession. I believe, thinking about my films, that hey are based not so much on pursuit as on a search. If we are looking or something, the labyrinth is the most favourable location for the earch. I do not know why, but my films are all for the most part a hysical search.

You reflect about your work a great deal. . . .

Never *a posteriori*. I think about each of my films when I am preparing for them. I do an enormous amount of preparation for each film nd I set aside the clearest sketch when starting. What is marvellous bout the cinema, what makes it superior to the theatre, is that it has any elements that may conquer us but may also enrich us, offer us a fe impossible anywhere else. The cinema should always be the discovery of something. I believe that the cinema should be essentially oetic; that is why, during the shooting and not during the preparation, try to plunge myself into a poetic development, which differs from arrative development and dramatic development. But, in reality, I am man of ideas; yes, above all else – I am even more a man of ideas than moralist, I suppose.

Do you believe it is possible to have a form of tragedy without nelodrama?

Yes, but it is very difficult. For any author in the Anglo-Saxon radition, it is very difficult. Shakespeare never managed it. It is possible, but up to the present no one has succeeded. In my cultural tradion, tragedy cannot escape from melodrama. We may always draw om tragic elements and perhaps even the grandeur of tragedy but lodrama is always inherent in the Anglo-Saxon cultural universe. re's no doubt about it.

Is it correct that your films never correspond to what you were thinkin of doing before starting them? Because of producers, etc.

No, in reality, in what concerns me, creation, I must say that I ar constantly changing. At the beginning, I have a basic notion of wha the final aspect of the film will be, more or less. But each day, ever moment, one changes or modifies because of the expression in a actress's eyes or the position of the sun. I am not in the habit c preparing a film and then setting myself to make it. I prepare a film bu I have no intention of making *this* film. The preparation serves t liberate me, so that I may work in my fashion; thinking of bits of filr and of the results they will give; and there are parts that deceive m because I haven't conceived them in a complete enough way. I do nc know what word to use, because I am afraid of pompous words when talk about making a film. The degree of concentration I use in a worl that I create, whether this be for thirty seconds or for two hours, is ver high; that is why, when I am shooting, I have a lot of trouble sleeping This is not because I am preoccupied but because, for me, this worl has so much reality that closing my eyes is not sufficient to make disappear. It represents a terrible intensity of feeling. If I shoot in royal location I sense and I see this site in so violent a way that, now when I see these places again, they are similar to tombs, completel dead. There are spots in the world that are, to my eyes, cadavers; tha is because I have already shot there – for me, they are completel finished. Jean Renoir said something that seems to be related to tha 'We should remind people that a field of wheat painted by Van Gog can arouse a stronger emotion than a field of wheat in nature.' It important to recall that art surpasses reality. Film becomes anothe reality. Apropos, I admire Renoir's work very much even though min doesn't please him at all. We are good friends and, truthfully, one c the things I regret is that he doesn't like his films for the same reason do. His films appear marvellous to me because what I admire mo in an *auteur* is authentic sensitivity. I attach no importance to wheth or not a film is a technical *success*: moreover, films that lack th genre of sensitivity may not be judged on the same level with technic or aesthetic knowingness. But the cinema, the true cinema, is a poet expression and Renoir is one of the rare poets. Like Ford, it is in h style. Ford is a poet. A comedian. Not for women, of course, but fc men.

Apart from Ford and Renoir, who are the cinéastes *you admire?*

Always the same ones; I believe that on this point I am not v original. The one who pleases me most of all is Griffith. I think h ne best director in the history of the cinema. The best, much better nan Eisenstein. And, for all that, I admire Eisenstein very much.

What about the letter Eisenstein sent you when you had not yet tarted in the cinema?

It was apropos *Ivan the Terrible.*

It appears that you said his film was like something by Michael Curtiz. . . .

No. What happened is that I wrote a criticism of *Ivan the Terrible* or a newspaper and, one day, I received a letter from Eisenstein, a etter that came from Russia and ran to forty pages. Well, I answered im and in this fashion an exchange began that made us friends by orrespondence. But I said nothing that could be seen as drawing a arallel between him and Curtiz. That would not be just. *Ivan the Terrible* is the worst film of a great *cinéaste.*

It's that I judged Eisenstein on his own level and not in a way that ould be appropriate to a minor *cinéaste.* His drama was, above all, olitical. It had nothing to do with his having to tell a story that he idn't want to tell. It was because, in my opinion, he was not a director f historical films. I think the Russians have a tendency to be more cademic when they deal with another period. They become rhetoricians, and academicians, in the worst sense of the word.

In your films, one has the sensation that real space is never respected: seems not to interest you. . . .

The fact that I make no use of it doesn't in the least signify that it oesn't please me. In other terms, there are many elements of the nematographic language that I do not use, but that is not because I ave something against them. It seems to me that the field of action in hich I have my experiences is one that is least known, and my duty to explore it. But that does not mean to say that it is, for me, the best nd only – or that I deviate from a normal conception of space, in elation to the camera. I believe that the artist should explore his eans of expression.

In reality, the cinema, with the exception of a few little tricks that on't go very far, has not advanced for more than thirty years. The nly changes are with respect to the subjects of films. I see that there re directors, full of future, sensitive, who explore new themes, but I e no one who attacks form, the manner of saying things. That seems interest no one. They resemble each other very much in terms of yle.

You must work very quickly. In twenty-five years of cinema, you have

Lady from Shanghai: Welles and Rita Hayworth

made ten films, you have acted in thirty, you have made a series of ver long programmes for television, you have acted and directed in th theatre, you have done narrations for other films and, in addition, yo have written thirty scenarios. Each of them must have taken you mor than six months.

Several of them even longer. There are those that took me two year but that is because I set them aside from time to time in order to d something else and picked them up again afterwards. But it is also tru that I write very rapidly.

You write them completely, with dialogue?

I always begin with the dialogue. And I do not understand how or dares to write action before dialogue. It's a very strange conception. know that in theory the word is secondary in cinema but the secret c my work is that everything is based on the word. I do not make siler films. I must begin with what the characters say. I must know wha they say before seeing them do what they do.

However, in your films the visual part is essential.

Yes, but I couldn't arrive at it without the solidity of the word tak

ady from Shanghai: Welles, Hayworth, Everett Sloane

ɩs a basis for constructing the images. What happens is that when the isual components are shot the words are obscured. The most classical xample is *Lady From Shanghai*. The scene in the aquarium was so ;ripping visually that no one heard what was being said. And what vas said was, for all that, the marrow of the film. The subject was so edious that I said to myself, 'This calls for something beautiful to look t.' Assuredly, the scene was very beautiful. The first ten minutes of the ılm did not please me at all. When I think of them I have the impression t wasn't me that made them. They resemble any Hollywood film.

I believe you know the story of *Lady From Shanghai*. I was working n that spectacular theatre idea 'Around the World in 80 Days', which vas originally to be produced by Mike Todd. But, overnight, he went ankrupt and I found myself in Boston on the day of the première, nable to collect my costumes from the station because 50,000 dollars vas due. Without that money we couldn't open. At that time I was lready separated from Rita; we were no longer even speaking. I did ɔt intend to do a film with her. From Boston I got in touch with ırry Cohn, then director of Columbia, who was in Hollywood, and I d to him, 'I have an extraordinary story for you if you send me

50,000 dollars, by telegram in one hour, on account, and I will sign contract to make it.' Cohn asked, 'What story?' I was telephoning fro the theatre box-office; beside it was a pocket books display and I gav him the title of one of them: *Lady From Shanghai.* I said to him, 'Bu the novel and I'll make the film.' An hour later we received the money Later I read the book and it was horrible so I set myself, top speed, t write a story. I arrived in Hollywood to make the film with a very sma budget and in six weeks of shooting. But I wanted more money for m theatre. Cohn asked me why I didn't use Rita. She said she would b very pleased. I gave her to understand that the character was not sympathetic one, that she was a woman who killed and this might hur her image as a star in the public eye. Rita was set on making this film and instead of costing 350,000 dollars, it became a two-million-dolla film. Rita was very co-operative. The person who was horrified o seeing the film was Cohn.

How do you work with actors?

I give them a great deal of freedom and, at the same time, the feelin of precision. It's a strange combination. In other words, physically and in the way they develop, I demand the precision of ballet. But thei way of acting comes directly from their own ideas as much as fron mine. When the camera begins to roll, I do not improvise visually. I this realm, everything is prepared. But I work very freely with th actors. I try to make their life pleasant.

Your cinema is essentially dynamic. . . .

I believe that the cinema should be dynamic although I suppose an artist will defend his own style. For me, the cinema is a slice of life i movement that is projected on a screen; it is not a frame. I do no believe in the cinema unless there is movement on the screen. This i why I am not in agreement with certain directors, whom, however, admire, who content themselves with a static cinema. For me, thes are dead images. I hear the noise of the projector behind me, and whe I see these long, long walks along streets, I am always waiting to hea the director's voice saying, 'Cut!'

The only director who does not move either his camera or his actor very much, and in whom I believe, is John Ford. He succeeds in makin me believe in his films even though there is little movement in them But with the others I always have the impression that they are des perately trying to make Art. However, they should be making dram and drama should be full of life. The cinema, for me, is essentially dramatic medium, not a literary one.

That is why your mise en scène *is lively: it is the meeting of two mo ents, that of the actors and that of the camera. Out of this flows an nguish that reflects modern life. . . .*

I believe that that corresponds to my vision of the world; it reflects at sort of vertigo, uncertainty, lack of stability, the *mélange* of movement and tension that is our universe. And the cinema should express at. Since cinema has the pretension of being an art, it should be, bove all, film, and not the sequel to another, more literary, medium f expression.

Herman G. Weinberg said, while speaking of Mr Arkadin, *'In Orson Velles's films, the spectator cannot sit back in his seat and relax; on the ontrary he must meet the film at least half-way in order to decipher what happening, practically every second; if not, everything is lost.'*

All my films are like that. There are certain *cinéastes*, excellent ones, ho present everything so explicitly, so clearly, that in spite of the reat visual power contained in their films one follows them effortlessly I refer only to the narrative thread. I am fully aware that, in my films, demand a very specific interest on the part of the public. Without at attention, it is lost.

Lady From Shanghai *is a story that, filmed by another director, ould more likely have been based on sexual questions. . . .*

You mean that another director would have made it more obvious. do not like to show sex on the screen crudely. Not because of morality r puritanism; my objection is of a purely aesthetic order. In my pinion, there are two things that can absolutely not be carried to the creen: the realistic presentation of the sexual act and praying to God. never believe an actor or actress who pretends to be completely volved in the sexual act if it is too literal, just as I can never believe n actor who wants to make me believe he is praying. These are two ings that, for me, immediately evoke the presence of a projector nd a white screen, the existence of a series of technicians and a irector who is saying, 'Good. Cut.' And I imagine them in the process f preparing for the next shot. As for those who adopt a mystical ance and look fervently at the spotlights. . . .

For all that, my illusion almost never ends when I see a film. While lming, I think of someone like myself: I use all my skill in order to rce this person to want to watch the film with the closest attention. I ant him to believe what is there on the screen; this means that one ould create a real world there. I place my dramatic vision of a haracter in the world . . . if not, the film is something dead. What there on the screen is nothing but shadows. Something even more dead an words.

Do you like comedy?

I have written at least five scenarios for comedy and in the theatre have done more comedies than dramas. Comedy fills me with enthusiasm but I have never succeeded in getting a film producer to let m make one. One of the best things I did for television was a programm in the genre of comedy. For example, I like Hawks's comedies ver much. I even wrote about twenty-five minutes of one of them. It wa called *I Was a Male War Bride*. The scenarist fell ill and I wrote almos a third of the film.

Have you written scenarios of comedies with the intention of makin them?

I believe the best of my comedies is *Operation Cinderella*. It tells o the occupation of a small Italian town (which was previously occupie by the Saracens, the Moors, the Normans and, during the last war, b the English and, finally, the Americans) by a Hollywood film compan and this new occupation unfolds exactly like a military operation. Th lives of all the inhabitants of the town are changed during the shootin of the film. It's a gross farce. I want very much to do a comedy for th cinema.

In a certain sense, *Quixote* is a comedy, and I put a lot of comedy i all of my films but it is a genre of comedy that – and I regret to tell yo this because it is a weakness – is understood only by Americans, t the exclusion of spectators in other countries, whatever they may b There are scenes that, seen in other countries, awake not the slighte smile and that, seen by Americans, immediately appear in a comi vein. *The Trial* is full of humour, but the Americans are the only one to understand its amusing side. This is where my nationality come through: my farces are not universal enough. Many are the argumen I've had with actors due to the fact that scenes are posed in absolu forms of comedy and only at the last five minutes do I change the into drama. This is my method of working: showing the amusing sid of things and not showing the sad side until the last possible secon

What happened when you sold the subject of Monsieur Verdoux *t Chaplin?*

I never argued with Chaplin over *Monsieur Verdoux*. What annoy me is that now he pretends that he did not buy this subject from me. A an actor, Chaplin is very good, sensational. But in the comic cinema prefer Buster Keaton. There is a man of the cinema who is not only a excellent actor but an excellent director, which Chaplin is not. An Keaton always has fabulous ideas. In *Limelight*, there was a te minute scene between the two of them. Chaplin was excellent an

Keaton sensational. It was the most successful thing he had done in the ourse of his career. Chaplin cut almost the entire scene, because he nderstood who, of the two, had completely dominated it.

There is a kinship between your work and the works of certain authors f the modern theatre, like Becket, Ionesco and others . . . what is called he theatre of the absurd.

Perhaps, but I would eliminate Ionesco because I do not admire him. When I directed *Rhinoceros* in London, with Laurence Olivier in the rincipal role, as we rehearsed the work from day to day it pleased me ess. I believe that there is nothing inside it. Nothing at all. This kind of heatre comes out of all types of expression, all types of art of a certain poch, is thus forged by the same world as my films. The things this heatre is composed of are the same as are composed in my films, without this theatre's being in my cinema or without my cinema's being n this theatre. It is the manner of our times. There is where the oincidence comes from.

There are two types of artists: for example, Velazquez and Goya; one isappears from the picture, the other is present in it. Similarly you have 'an Gogh and Cézanne. . . .

I see what you mean. It's very clear.

It seems to me that you are on the Goya side.

Doubtless. But I very much prefer Velazquez. There's no comarison between one and the other, as far as being artists is concerned. As I prefer Cézanne to Van Gogh.

And between Tolstoy and Dostoievsky?

I prefer Tolstoy.

But as an artist. . . .

Yes, as an artist. But I deny that, for I do not correspond to my astes. I know what I'm doing and when I recognize it in other works ny interest is diminished. The things that resemble me the least are the hings that interest me the most. For me Velazquez is the Shakespeare f painters and, for all that, he has nothing in common with my way f working.

What do you think of what is called modern cinema?

I like certain young French *cinéastes*, much more than the Italians.

Did you like L'Année Dernière à Marienbad*?*

No. I know that this film pleased you; not me. I held on up to the ourth reel and after that I left at a run. It reminded me too much of *'ogue* magazine.

How do you see the development of the cinema?

I don't see it. I rarely go to the movies. There are two kinds of writers the writer who reads everything of interest that is published, exchanges letters with other writers, and others who absolutely do not read their contemporaries. I am among the latter. I go to the movies very rarely and this is not because I don't like it, it is because it gives me no enjoyment at all. I do not think I am very intelligent about films. There are works that I know to be good but which I cannot stand.

It was said that you were going to make Crime and Punishment. *What became of this project?*

Someone wanted me to do it. I thought about it, but I like the book too much. In the end, I decided that I could do nothing and the idea o being content to illustrate it did not please me at all. I don't mean to say by that that the subject was beneath me, what I mean is that I could bring nothing to it. I could only give it actors and images and, when can only do that, the cinema does not interest me. I believe you mus say something new about a book, otherwise it is better not to touch it

Aside from that, I consider it to be a very difficult work, because, in my opinion, it is not completely comprehensible outside of its own time and country. The psychology of this man and this detective are so Russian, so nineteenth-century Russian, that one could never find them elsewhere; I don't believe that the public would be able to follow it all the way.

There is, in Dostoievsky, an analysis of justice, of the world, that is very close to yours.

Perhaps too close. My contribution would most likely be limited The only thing I could do is to direct. I like to make films in which I can express myself as *auteur* rather than as interpreter. I do not share Kafka's point of view in *The Trial*. I believe that he is a good writer but Kafka is not the extraordinary genius that people today see him as That is why I was not concerned about excessive fidelity and could make a film by Welles. If I could make four films a year, I would surely do *Crime and Punishment*. But as it costs me a great deal to convince producers I try to choose what I film very carefully.

With you, one seems to find, at the same time, the Brechtian tendency and the Stanislavsky tendency.

All I can say is that I did my apprenticeship in Stanislavsky's orbit; worked with his actors and found them very easy to direct. I do no allude to 'Method' actors; that's something else altogether. But Stanislavsky was marvellous. As for Brecht, he was a great friend to me

We worked together on *Galileo Galilei*. In reality he wrote it for me. Not for me to act in, but in order for me to direct it.

How was Brecht?

Terribly nice. He had an extraordinary brain. One could see very well that he had been educated by the Jesuits. He had the type of disciplined brain characteristic of Jesuit education. Instinctively, he was more of an anarchist than a Marxist, but he believed himself a perfect Marxist. When I said to him one day, while we were talking about *Galileo*, that he had written a perfectly anti-communist work, he became nearly aggressive. I answered him, 'But this Church you describe has to be Stalin and not the Pope, at this time. You have made something resolutely anti-Soviet!'

What relationship do you see between your work as a film director and as a theatre director?

My relationships with these two milieux are very different. I don't believe that they are in intimate rapport one with the other. Perhaps in me, as a man, that relationship exists, but technical solutions are so different for each of them.

In the theatre there are 1,500 cameras rolling at the same time – in he Brechtian idea of theatre; that particularly withdrawn form has never been appropriate to my character. But I have always made a terrible effort to recall to the public, at each instant, that it is in a theatre. I have never tried to bring it into the scene, I have rather tried to bring the scene to it. And that is the opposite of the cinema.

Perhaps there is a relationship in the way the actors are handled.

In the theatre there are 1,500 cameras rolling at the same time – in the cinema there is only one. That changes the whole aesthetic for the director.

Did Huston's Moby Dick, *on which you worked, please you?*

The novel pleases me very much but it doesn't please me as a novel so much as a drama. There are two very different things in the novel: that sort of pseudo-biblical element that is not very good, and also that curious nineteenth-century American element, of the apocalyptical genre, that can be rendered very well in the cinema.

In the scene you acted in the film – did you make any suggestions as to the way of handling it?

All we did was discuss the way in which it would be shot. You know that my speech is very long. It goes on throughout a full reel, and we never rehearsed it. I arrived on the set already made-up and dressed. I got up on the platform and we shot it in one take. We did it using only one camera angle. And that is one of Huston's merits, because another director would have said, 'Let's do it from another angle and see what we get.' He said, 'Good,' and my role in the film ended right there!

You are in the process of preparing for a film on bullfighting.

Yes, but a film about the amateurs of bullfighting, the following . . . I think that the true event in the *corrida* is the arena itself – but one cannot do a film about it. From the cinematographic point of view the most exciting thing about it is the atmosphere. The *corrida* is something that already possesses a well defined personality. The cinema can do nothing to render it dramatic. All one may do is photograph it. Actually, my biggest preoccupation is knowing that Rosi is already in the process of shooting while I have put in four years, off and on, writing my scenario. Because of him, finding the necessary money will be more difficult: they'll say to me, 'We already have a film about bullfighting, made by a serious *cinéaste*; who wants one more?' However, I hope I will succeed in making this film, but I still don't know how I'm going to find the money. Rosi shot something last year at Pamplona in 16 mm. He showed it to Rizzoli, and said, 'Look at this beautiful thing,' and Rizzoli gave him *carte blanche*. Now it's only a matter of knowing whether it will be a good film or a bad film. It is better for me that the film be good. If it fails, I will have even more trouble raising the funds.

There is talk from time to time of your first sojourn in Spain, before the Civil War. . . .

When I arrived in Spain, for the first time, I was seventeen years old and had already worked in Ireland as an actor. I only stayed in the south, in Andalusia. In Seville, I lived in the Triana section. I was writing detective stories: I spent only two days a week on this and it brought in three hundred dollars. With this money I was a *grand seigneur* in Seville. There were so many people thrilled by the *corrida* and I caught the virus myself. I paid the novice fee at several *corridas* and thus was able to *debut* – on the posters I was called 'The American'. My greatest thrill was being able to practise the *métier* of *torero* three or four times without having to pay. I came to the realization that I was not good as a *torero* and decided to apply myself to writing. At that time I hardly thought of the theatre and still less of the cinema.

You said one day that you have had a great deal of difficulty finding the money to make your films, that you have spent more time struggling to get this money than working as an artist. How is this battle at the moment?

More bitter than ever. Worse than ever. Very difficult. I have already said that I do not work enough. I am frustrated, do you understand? And I believe that my work shows that I do not do enough filming. My cinema is perhaps too explosive, because I wait too long before I speak. It's terrible. I have bought little cameras in order to make a film if I can find the money. I will shoot it in 16 mm. The cinema is a *métier* . . . nothing can compare to the cinema. The cinema belongs to our times. It is 'the thing' to do. During the shooting of *The Trial*, I had some marvellous days. It was an amusement, happiness. You cannot imagine what I felt.

When I make a film or at the time of my theatrical premières, the critics habitually say, 'This work is not as good as the one of three years ago.' And if I look for the criticism of that one, three years back, I find an unfavourable review that says that that isn't as good as what I did three years earlier. And so it goes. I admit that experiences can be false but I believe that it is also false to want to be fashionable. If one is fashionable for the greatest part of one's career, one will produce second-class work. Perhaps by chance one will arrive at being a success but this means that one is a follower and not an innovator. An artist should lead, blaze trails.

What is serious is that in countries where English is spoken, the role played by criticism concerning serious works of cinema is very important. Given the fact that one cannot make films in competition with Doris Day, what is said by reviews such as *Sight and Sound* is the only reference.

Things are going particularly badly in my own country. *Touch of Evil* never had a first-run, never had the usual presentation to the press and was not the object of any critical writing in either the weeklies, the reviews or the daily papers. It was considered to be too bad. When the representative from Universal wanted to exhibit it at the Brussels Fair in 1958, he was told that it wasn't a good enough film for a festival. He answered that, in any case, it must be put on the programme. It went unnoticed and was sent back. The film took the *grand prix*, but it was sent back just the same.

Do you consider yourself a moralist?

Yes, but against morality. Most of the time that may appear paradoxical, but the things I love in painting, in music, in literature, represent only my penchant for what is my opposite. And moralists bore me very much. However, I'm afraid I am one of them!

It is not so much a question of a moralist's attitude but rather an ethic that you adopt in the face of the world.

My two Shakespearian films are made from an ethical point of view. I believe I have never made a film without having a solid ethical point of view about its story. Morally speaking, there is no ambiguity in what I do.

But an ambiguous point of view is necessary. These days, the world is made that way.

But that is the way the world appears to us. It is not a true ambiguity: it's like a larger screen. A kind of a moral CinemaScope. I believe it is necessary to give all the characters their best arguments, in order that they may defend themselves, including those I disagree with. To them as well, I give the best defensive arguments I can imagine. I offer them the same scope for expression as I would a sympathetic character.

That's what gives this impression of ambiguity: my being chivalrous to people whose behaviour I do not approve of. The characters are ambiguous but the significance of the work is not. I do not want to resemble the majority of Americans, who are demagogues and rhetoricians. This is one of America's great weaknesses, and rhetoric is one of the greatest weaknesses of American artists; above all, those of my generation. Miller, for example, is terribly rhetorical.

What is the problem in America?

If I speak to you of the things that are wrong it won't be the obvious ones; those are similar to what is wrong in France, in Italy or in Spain; we know them all. In American art the problem, or better, one of the problems, is the betrayal of the Left by the Left, self-betrayal. In one sense, by stupidity, by orthodoxy and because of slogans; in another, by simple betrayal. We are very few in our generation who have not betrayed our position, who have not given other people's names. . . .

That is terrible. It can never be undone. I don't know how one starts again after such a betrayal, one that, however, differs enormously from this, for example: a Frenchman who collaborated with the Gestapo in order to save his wife's life – that is another kind of collaboration. What is so bad about the American Left is that it betrayed in order to save its swimming pools. There was no American Right in my generation. Intellectually it didn't exist. There were only Leftists and they mutually betrayed each other. The Left was not destroyed by McCarthy: it demolished itself, ceding to a new generation of Nihilists. That's what happened.

You can't call it 'Fascism'. I believe that the term 'Fascism' should only be used in order to define a quite precise political attitude. It would be necessary to find a new word in order to define what is happening in America. Fascism must be born out of chaos. And America is not, as I know it, in chaos. The social structure is not in a state of dissolution. No, it doesn't correspond at all to the true definition of Fascism. I believe it is two simple, obvious things: the technological society is not accustomed to living with its own tools. That's what counts. We speak of them, we use them but we don't know how to live with them. The other thing is the prestige of the people responsible for the technological society. In this society the men who direct and the savants who represent technique do not leave room for the artist who favours the human being. In reality, they use him only for decoration.

Hemingway says, in *The Green Hills of Africa*, that America is a country of adventure and, if the adventure disappears there, any American who possesses this primitive spirit must go elsewhere to seek adventure: Africa, Europe, etc. . . . It is an intensely romantic point of view. There is some truth in it, but if it is so intensely romantic it is because there is still an enormous quantity of adventure in America. In the cinema, you cannot imagine all that one may do in it. All I need is a job in cinema: for someone to give me a camera. There is nothing dishonourable about working in America. The country is full of possibilities for expressing what is happening all over the world. What really exists is an enormous compromise. The ideal American type is perfectly expressed by the Protestant, individualist, anticonformist, and this is the type that is in the process of disappearing. In reality there are few left.

What was your relationship with Hemingway?

My relationship with Hemingway has always been very amusing. The first time we met was when I had been called to read the narration for a film that he and Joris Ivens had made about the war in Spain; it was called *Spanish Earth*. Arriving, I came upon Hemingway, who was in the process of drinking a bottle of whisky; I had been handed a set of lines that were too long, dull, had nothing to do with his style, which is always so concise and so economical. There were lines as pompous and complicated as this: 'Here are the faces of men who are close to death', and this was to be read at a moment when one saw faces on the screen that were so much more eloquent. I said to him, 'Mr Hemingway, it would be better if one saw the faces all alone, without commentary.'

This didn't please him at all, and since I had, a short time before, just directed the Mercury Theatre, which was a sort of *avant-garde* theatre, he thought I was some kind of faggot and said, 'You—effeminate boys of the theatre, what do you know about real war?'

Taking the bull by the horns, I began to make effeminate gestures and I said to him, 'Mister Hemingway, how strong you are and how big you are!' That enraged him and he picked up a chair; I picked up another, and right there, in front of the images of the Spanish Civil War as they marched across the screen, we had a terrible scuffle. It was something marvellous: two guys like us in front of these images representing people in the act of struggling and dying . . . we ended by giving each other accolades and drinking a bottle of whisky. We have spent our lives having long periods of friendship and others during which we barely spoke. I have never been able to avoid gently making fun of him, and this no one ever did – everyone treated him with the greatest respect.

As an artist and as a member of a certain generation, do you feel isolated?

I have always felt isolated. I believe that any good artist feels isolated. And I must think that I am a good artist, for otherwise I would not be able to work and I beg your pardon for taking the liberty of believing this; if someone wants to direct a film, he must think that he is good. A good artist should be isolated. If he isn't isolated, something is wrong.

These days, it would be impossible to present the Mercury Theatre.

Completely impossible for financial reasons. The Mercury Theatre was possible only because I was earning three thousand dollars a week on the radio and spending two thousand to support the theatre. At that time, it was still cheap to support a theatre. I had formidable actors. And what was most exciting about this Mercury Theatre was that it was a theatre on Broadway, not 'off'. Today, one might have a theatre off Broadway, but that's another thing.

What characterized the Mercury Theatre was that it was next door to another where they were doing a musical comedy, near a commercial theatre, it was in the theatre centre. Part of the neighbouring bill of fare was the Group Theatre which was the official theatre of the Left: we were in contact without having an official relationship; we were of the same generation, although not on the same path. The whole thing gave the New York of that time an extraordinary vitality. The quality of actors and that of spectators is no longer what it was in those marvellous years. The best theatre should be in the centre of everything.

Does that explain your permanent battle to remain in the milieu of the cinema and not outside the industry?

I may be rejected, but I always want to be right in the centre. If I am isolated, it is because I am obliged to be, not because I want to be. I am always aiming for the centre. I fail, but that is what I try for.

Are you thinking of returning to Hollywood?

Not at the moment. But who knows what may change at the next instant? . . . I am dying to work there because of the technicians, who are marvellous. They truly represent a director's dream.

A certain anti-Fascist attitude can be found in your films. . . .

There is more than one French intellectual who believes that I am a Fascist . . . it's idiotic, but that's what they write. What happens with these French intellectuals is that they confuse my physique as an actor with my ideas as an *auteur*. As an actor I always play a certain type of role: kings, great men, etc. This is not because I think them the only persons in the world who are worth the trouble. My physique does not permit me to play other roles. No one would believe in a defenceless, humble person played by me. But they take this to be a projection of my own personality. I hope that the great majority at least considers it obvious that I am anti-Fascist. . . .

True Fascism is always confused with Futurism's early fascistic mystique. I allude to the first generation of Italian Fascism, which had a way of speaking that disappeared as soon as the true Fascism imposed itself, because it was an idiotic romanticism, like that of d'Annunzio and others. That is what disappeared. And that is what the French critics are talking about.

True Fascism is gangsterism of the low-born middle class, lamentably organized by . . . we all know what Fascism is. It is very clear. It is amusing to see how the Russians have been mistaken about the subject of *Touch of Evil*. They have attacked it pitilessly, as if it were a question of the veritable decadence of Western civilization. They were not content to attack what I showed: they attacked me too.

I believe that the Russians didn't understand the words, or some other thing. What is disastrous, in Russia, is that they are completely in the Middle Ages, the Middle Ages in their most rigid aspect. No one thinks for himself. It is very sad. This orthodoxy has something terrible about it. They live by slogans they have inherited. No one any longer knows what these slogans signify.

What will your Falstaff *be like?*

I don't know . . . I hope it will be good. All I can say is that from the visual point of view it will be very modest and, I hope, at the same time satisfying and correct. But as I see it, it is essentially a human story and I hope that a good number of stupid cinema people will feel cheated. That is because, as I just said, I consider that this film should be very modest from the visual point of view. Which doesn't mean it will be visually non-existent but rather that it will not be loud on this level. It

Othello: Welles, with Micheál MacLiammoir's Iago

concerns a story about three or four people and these should, therefore dominate completely. I believe I shall use more close-ups. This wil really be a film completely in the service of the actors.

You are often accused of being egocentric. When you appear as a actor in your films, it is said that the camera is, above all, in the service o your personal exhibition. . . . For example, in Touch of Evil *the shootin angle moves from a general shot to a close-up in order to catch you first appearance on getting out of the car.*

Yes, but that is the story, the subject. I wouldn't act a role if it wa not felt as dominating the whole story. I do not think it is just to sa that I use the camera to my profit and not to the profit of the othe actors. It's not true. Although they will say it even more about *Falstaff* but it is precisely because in the film I am playing Falstaff, not Hotspur

At this time I think and rethink, above all, of the world in which th story unfolds, of the appearance of the film. The number of sets I shal be able to build will be so limited that the film will have to be resolutel anti-Baroque. It will have to have numerous rather formal general sets that one can see at eye level, like wall frescoes. It is a big problen

'himes at Midnight: Welles as Falstaff

:reating a world in period costumes. In this genre, it is difficult to get feeling of real life; few films achieve it.

Falstaff should be very bare on the visual level because above all it is very real human story, very comprehensible and very adaptable to nodern tragedy. And nothing should come between the story and the lialogue. The visual part of this story should exist as a background, as omething secondary. Everything of importance in the film should be ound on the faces; in these faces that whole universe I was speaking of hould be found. I imagine that it will be 'the' film of my life in terms of lose-ups. Theoretically, I am against close-ups of all types, although I onsider few theories as given and am for remaining very free. I am esolutely against close-ups, but I am convinced that this story equires them.

Why this objection to close-ups?

I find it marvellous that the public may select, with its eyes, what it vants to see of a shot. I don't like to force it, and the use of the close-up mounts to forcing it: you can see nothing else. In *Kane*, for example, ou must have seen that there were very few close-ups, hardly any.

There are perhaps six in the whole film. But a story like *Falstaff* demands them, because the moment we step back and separate ourselves from the faces, we see the people in period costumes and many actors in the foreground. The closer we are to the face the more universal it becomes; *Falstaff* is a sombre comedy, the story of the betrayal of friendship.

What pleases me in *Falstaff* is that the project has interested me as an actor although I am rarely interested in something for the cinema in terms of being an actor. I am happy when I do not perform. And *Falstaff* is one of the rare things that I wish to achieve as an actor. There are only two stories I wish to do as an actor that I have written. In *The Trial* I absolutely did not want to perform and I only did so because of not having found an actor who could take the part. All those we asked refused.

At the beginning you said you would play the part of the priest. . . .

I shot it, but, as we hadn't found an actor for the role of the lawyer I cut the sequences in which I appeared as a priest and started shooting again. *Falstaff* is an actor's film. Not only my role but all the others are favourable for showing a good actor's worth. My *Othello* is more successful in the theatre than on film. We shall see what happens with *Falstaff*, which is the best role that Shakespeare ever wrote. It is a character as great as Don Quixote. If Shakespeare had done nothing but that magnificent creation, it would suffice to make him immortal. I wrote the scenario under the inspiration of three works in which he appears, one other in which he is spoken of, and completed it with things found in still another. Thus, I worked with five of Shakespeare's works. But, naturally, I wrote a story about Falstaff, about his friendship with the prince and his rejection when the prince becomes king. I have great hopes for this film.

There is a line spoken by John Foster to his banker, which we would like very much to hear you explain: 'I could have been a great man, if I hadn't been so rich.'

The whole story is in that. Anything at all may destroy greatness: a woman, illness, riches. My hatred of wealth in itself is not an obsession. I do not believe that wealth is the only enemy of greatness. If he had been poor, Kane would not have been a great man but one thing is sure and that is that he would have been a successful man. He thinks that success brings greatness. As for that, it is the character that says it, not I. Kane achieves a certain class but never greatness.

It isn't because everything seems easy to him. That is an excuse he gives himself. But the film doesn't say that. Obviously, since he is the head of one of the biggest fortunes in the world, things become easier, but his greatest error was that of the American plutocrats of those years, who believed that money automatically conferred a certain stature to a man. Kane is a man who truly belongs to his time. That type of man hardly exists anymore. These were the plutocrats who believed they could be President of the United States, if they wanted to. They also believed they could buy anything. It wasn't even necessary to be intelligent to see that it isn't always like that.

Are they more realistic?

It's not a question of realism. That type of plutocrat no longer exists. Things have changed a great deal, above all economic structures. Very few rich men today succeed in retaining absolute control of their own money: their money is controlled by others. It is, like many other things, a question of organization. They are prisoners of their money. And I don't say this from a sentimental point of view; there are no longer anything but boards of directors and the participation of diverse opinions . . . they are no longer free to commit the sort of follies that used to be possible. The moment has passed for this type of egocentric plutocrat, in the same way that this type of newspaper owner has disappeared.

What is very specific about Kane's personality is that he never earned money; he spent his life doing nothing but spending it. He did not belong to that category of rich men who made fortunes: he only spent it. Kane didn't even have the responsibility of the true capitalist.

Did Citizen Kane *bring in a lot of money?*

No, it's not a question of that. The film went well. But my problems with Hollywood started before I got there. The real problem was that contract, which gave me, free and clear, *carte blanche* and which had been signed before I went out there. I had too much power. At that time I was faced with a plot from which I never recovered, because I have never had an enormous box-office success. If you have such success, from that instant on you are given everything!

I had luck as no one had; afterwards, I had the worst bad luck in the history of the cinema, but that is in the order of things: I had to pay for having had the best luck in the history of the cinema. Never has a man been given so much power in the Hollywood system. An absolute power. And artistic control.

There are cinéastes, *in Europe, who possess this power.*

But they don't possess the American technical arsenal, which is a grandiose thing. The man who pushes the camera, those who change the lights, the one who handles the crane – they have children at the

Touch of Evil: Welles, Akim Tamiroff

University. You are side by side with men who don't feel themselves to be workers but who think of themselves as very capable and very well paid craftsmen. That makes an enormous difference; enormous.

I could never have done all that I did in *Touch of Evil* elsewhere. And it is not only a question of technique; it essentially concerns the human competence of the men with whom I worked. All this stems from the economic security they enjoy, from the fact that they are well paid, from the fact that they do not think of themselves as belonging to another class.

Throughout the entire European cinema industry, to a greater or lesser degree, one feels that there is a great barrier posed by educational differences. In all European countries one is called 'Doctor', 'Professor', etc., if one has gone to a university; the great advantage in America is that there, at times, you find directors who are less learned than the man who pushes the camera. There is no 'professor'. Classes do not exist in the American cinema world. The pleasure one experiences working with an American crew is something that has no equivalent on earth. But you pay a price for that. There are the producers, and that group is as bad as the technicians are good.

How did you shoot that very long sequence in Marcia's living-room during the interrogation of Sanchez?

In Europe, there are three cameramen as good as the American cameramen. The one who made *The Trial* with me is sensational. But what there isn't is someone capable of handling the crane. In America, this man has an enormous car; he is educated and he considers himself as important to the film as the cameraman himself. In that scene in Marcia's house there were about sixty chalk marks on the ground: that tells you how knowledgeable and intelligent the man who guides the camera must be in order to do well. At that moment, I am at his mercy, at the mercy of his precision. If he can't do it with assurance, the scene is impossible.

Was it really Charlton Heston who proposed you as director of Touch of Evil*?*

What happened is even more amusing. The scenario was offered to Charlton Heston who was told that it was by Orson Welles; at the other end of the line, Heston understood that I was to direct the film, in which case he was ready to shoot anything at all, no matter what, with me. Those at Universal did not clear up his misunderstanding; they hung up and automatically telephoned me and asked me to direct it. The truth is that Heston said, textually, this: 'I will work in any film at all directed by Orson Welles.' When they proposed that I direct the film I set only one condition: to write my own scenario! And I directed and wrote the film without getting a penny for it, since I was being paid as an actor.

In relation to the original novel, you made many changes. . . .

My God! I never read the novel; I only read Universal's scenario. Perhaps the novel made sense, but the scenario was ridiculous. It all took place in San Diego, not on the Mexican border, which completely changes the situation. I made Vargas a Mexican for political reasons: I wanted to show how Tijuana and the border towns are corrupted by all sorts of mish-mash – publicity more or less about American relations; that's the only reason.

What do you think of the American cinema, as seen from Europe?

I am surprised by the tendency of the serious critics to find elements of value only among the American directors of action films, while they find none in the American directors of historical films. Lubitsch, for example, is a giant. But he doesn't correspond to the taste of cinema aesthetes. Why? I know nothing about it. Besides, it doesn't interest me. But Lubitsch's talent and originality are stupefying.

And von Sternberg?

Admirable! He is the greatest exotic director of all time and one of the great lights.

Let's talk about other directors. What do you think of Arthur Penn? Have you seen The Left-Handed Gun*?*

I saw it first on television and then as cinema. It was better on television, more brutal. Besides, at that time Penn had more experience directing for television and so handled it better, but for cinema this experience went against him. I believe him to be a good theatre director, an admirable director of actresses – a very rare thing: very few *cinéastes* possess that quality.

I have seen nothing by the most recent generation, except for a sampling of the *avant-garde*. Among those whom I would call 'younger generation' Kubrick appears to me to be a giant.

But, for example, The Killing *was more or less a copy of* The Asphalt Jungle*?*

Yes, but *The Killing* was better. The problem of imitation leaves me indifferent, above all if the imitator succeeds in surpassing the model. For me, Kubrick is a better director than Huston. I haven't seen *Lolita* but I believe that Kubrick can do everything. He is a great director who has not yet made his great film. What I see in him is a talent not possessed by the great directors of the generation immediately preceding his, I mean Ray, Aldrich, etc. Perhaps this is because his temperament comes closer to mine.

And those of the older generation? Wyler, for example? and Hitchcock?

Hitchcock is an extraordinary director; William Wyler a brilliant producer.

How do you make this distinction between two men who are both called directors?

A producer doesn't make anything. He chooses the story, works on it with the scenarist, has a say in the distribution and, in the old sense of the American term producer, even decides on the camera angles, what sequences will be used. What is more, he defines the final form of the film. In reality, he is a sort of director's boss.

Wyler is this man. Only he's his own boss. His work, however, is better as boss than as director, given the fact that in that role he spends his clearest moments waiting, with the camera, for something to happen. He says nothing. He waits, as the producer waits in his office. He looks at twenty impeccable shots, seeking the one that has some-

Citizen Kane: Joseph Cotten, Welles

thing, and usually he knows how to choose the best one. As a director he is good but as a producer he is extraordinary.

According to you, the role of director consists in making something happen?

I do not like to set up very strict rules, but in the Hollywood system, the director has one job. In other systems he has another job. I am against absolute rules because even in the case of America we find marvellous films achieved under the absolute tyranny of the production system. There are even films much respected by film societies that weren't made by directors but by producers and scenarists. . . . Under the American system, no one is capable of saying whether a film was or was not directed by a director.

In an interview, John Houseman said that you got all the credit for Citizen Kane *and that this was unfair because it should have gone to Herman J. Mankiewicz, who wrote the scenario.*

He wrote several important scenes. (Houseman is an old enemy of mine.) I was very lucky to work with Mankiewicz: everything concerning Rosebud belongs to him. As for me, sincerely, he doesn't

Citizen Kane: Welles, Ruth Warrick

please me very much; he functions, it is true, but I have never had complete confidence in him. He serves as a hyphen between all the elements. I had, in return, the good fortune to have Gregg Toland, who is the best director of photography that ever existed, and I also had the luck to hit upon actors who had never worked in films before; not a single one of them had ever found himself in front of a camera until then. They all came from my theatre. I could never have made *Citizen Kane* with actors who were old hands at cinema, because they would have said right off, 'Just what do you think we're doing?' My being a newcomer would have put them on guard and, at the same time, would have made a mess of the film. It was possible because I had my own family, so to speak.

How did you arrive at Citizen Kane*'s cinematic innovations?*

I owe it to my ignorance. If this word seems inadequate to you replace it with innocence. I said to myself: this is what the camera should be really capable of doing, in a normal fashion. When we were on the point of shooting the first sequence, I said, 'Let's do that!' Gregg Toland answered that it was impossible. I came back with, 'We can always try; we'll soon see. Why not?' We had to have special lenses made because at that time there weren't any like those that exist today.

During the shooting, did you have the sensation of making such an important film?

I never doubted it for a single instant.

What is happening with your Don Quixote*? It was announced so long ago.*

It's really finished; it only needs about three weeks' work, in order o shoot several little things. What makes me nervous is launching it: I know that this film will please no one. This will be an execrated film. I need a big success before putting it in circulation. If *The Trial* had been a complete critical success, then I would have had the courage o bring out my *Don Quixote*. Things being what they are I don't know what to do: everyone will be enraged by this film.

How do you see the central character?

Exactly as Cervantes did, I believe. My film takes place in modern imes but the characters of Don Quixote and Sancho are exactly as hey were, at least, I repeat, to my way of thinking. This wasn't the case with Kafka; I use these two characters freely but I do it in the same spirit as Cervantes. They are not my characters, they are the Spanish writer's.

Why did you choose to film Don Quixote*?*

I started by making a half-hour television film out of it; I had just enough money to do it. But I fell so completely in love with my subject hat I gradually made it longer and continued to shoot depending on how much money I had. You might say that it grew as I made it. What happened to me is more or less what happened to Cervantes, who started to write a novella and ended up writing *Don Quixote*. It's a subject you can't let go of once you've started.

Will the film have the same scepticism as the novel?

Certainly! I believe that what happened to the book will happen to my film. You know that Cervantes started out to write a satire on books of chivalry and he ended up creating the most beautiful apology for them that can be found in literature. However, touching on the defence of that idea of chivalry, the film will be more sincere than the novel, even though today it is more anachronistic than when Cervantes was writing.

I myself appear in the character of Orson Welles, but Sancho and

Don Quixote say only the lines given them by Cervantes; I have pu no words in their mouths.

I do not think the film is less sceptical because I believe that, if w push the analysis to the end, Cervantes' scepticism was in part a attitude. His scepticism was an intellectual attitude: I believe that under the scepticism, there was a man who loved the knights as muc as Don Quixote himself. Above all, he was Spanish.

It is truly a difficult film. I should also say that it is too long; wha I am going to shoot will not complete the footage – I could make thre films out of the material that already exists. The film, in its first form was too commercial; it was conceived for television and I had t change certain things in order to make it more substantial. Th funniest thing about it is that it was shot with a crew of six people. M wife was script-girl, the chauffeur moved the lights around, I did th lighting and was second cameraman. It is only with the camera tha one can keep one's eye on everything like that.

Orson Welles: films as director

1941: *Citizen Kane*
1942: *The Magnificent Ambersons*
1943: *Journey into Fear* (completed and signed by Norman Foster
1946: *The Stranger*
1948: *Lady from Shanghai, Macbeth*
1952: *Othello*
1955: *Confidential Report*
1958: *Touch of Evil*
1962: *Le Procès (The Trial)*
1966: *Chimes at Midnight*
1968: *Une Histoire Immortelle*